MARRIAGE IN MOTION

Biblical Principles for Creating and
Sustaining a Healthy Marriage

BY
JOHN P. HOBBS

jhobbs@crossroadsnewnan.org

Lynchburg, Va.
www.liberty.edu/libertyuniversitypress

DEDICATION

I would like to thank my wife and children for putting up with all the hours I spent in front of the computer and my continual procrastination. Their love for me, and support of my desire to write this book has been a constant source of encouragement and strength. Thank you to Christy for guarding my time, to J.O. for pushing me forward, and to Crossroads Church for allowing me to develop and flesh out this material.

TABLE OF CONTENTS

INTRODUCTION. 7

CHAPTER 1 - COMMITMENT. 11

CHAPTER 2 - COMPATIBILITY. 29

CHAPTER 3 - COMMUNICATION. 49

CHAPTER 4 - COURTSHIP. 69

CHAPTER 5 - CONFLICT. 85

CHAPTER 6 - CONFESSION. 101

CHAPTER 7 - CLOSENESS. 115

CHAPTER 8 - CLEAVING. 133

CHAPTER 9 - CHEATING. 145

CHAPTER 10 - CHILDREN. 161

CONCLUSION. 173

ENDNOTES. 175

ABOUT THE AUTHOR. 179

INTRODUCTION

Marriage is the most mysterious relationship two human beings will ever know. It can be the most wonderful, exciting, fulfilling, life-giving, meaningful experience a person could ever have. And, it can be the most painful, exhausting, miserable, draining, frustrating experience anyone could imagine. I once heard someone say, "Marriage is the most perfect picture of heaven and hell we will know this side of eternity." Some might think this is a bit over dramatic, but I agree with it completely. Why does this particular relationship have such awesome potential for heavenly ecstasy and hellish agony? The answer is at least partially found in the unique covenant that binds the two participants. No other human relationship is defined by the words "till death do us part." For instance when two friends get tired of each other's company, one or the other can leave. If the friendship continues to deteriorate, it can be dissolved immediately by one or both of the parties. When a person becomes frustrated with a boss or co-worker, he can always tender his resignation. A teacher and her pupil only have to endure each other's company for so long before the semester mercifully ends. Good Christian people, who find themselves sitting on a pew every week with someone they believe even Jesus wouldn't like, can always find a new congregation in which to worship. The home of origin is a little more difficult because it lasts longer, but even in family relationships there is a light at the end of the tunnel called High School graduation. Marriage is the only human relationship designed to last forever.

The binding covenant is not the only factor that makes wedded bliss difficult. Usually the two individuals involved are as different as they can be. Take the two very different genders, male and female, and place them together. Already there is potential for disaster. In most cases this male and female have completely opposite personality types. Seldom have the couple been raised in similar families or taught compatible beliefs. Each person enters into this new relationship with unbelievable and unrealistic expectations that seem completely feasible in his/her own eyes. Neither of them may have had any training in anger management, communication skills or conflict resolution, and most have no experience or understanding when it comes to financial matters. To make it worse, probably in most cases neither of them had very good role models growing up. They may have a limited support system to turn to if things deteriorate.

One would think that Christian couples, having a common bond in Christ, would find married life easier to navigate. However, most statistics don't support that conclusion. Being a believer, and even being raised in the church, do not seem to be enough to create a happy, healthy marriage. These Christian couples face the same struggles as those who have not accepted Christ, and their belief system alone does not give them the marital direction that couples so desperately need to survive and thrive. The church, while all along insisting that divorce is wrong, has not done a very good job training couples to live a lifetime together.

"Marriage In Motion" was written as a tool for the local church to use in its effort to strengthening marriages. Biblically-based, Christ-centered material offers hope and direction to those who are struggling. The title represents the fact that marriages are constantly changing. Like riding a bicycle, it is impossible to just sit still. People are either going forward or they are going backward. Marriages are either getting better, or they are getting worse. They never remain the same. My hope is that this material will help many marriages move forward toward what God intends them to be.

Chapter 1

COMMITMENT

We live in a day and age that places very little emphasis on commitment. Seldom do we see someone devote thirty years of their life to one company and then retire any more. Professional athletes change uniforms sometimes yearly, depending on which team offers the largest contract. People hop from church to church looking for all the right ministries that can meet the needs of their family. Loyalty seems to be a thing of the past. That is certainly the case when it comes to marriage. In the pages that follow several topics will be covered, but none will be as important as the first. Every other area hinges on this one important issue -- commitment. When it comes to discussing marriage I can think of no better place to begin.

A Foundation of Faith

In America the divorce rate is about fifty percent; one out of every two marriages fail. The amazing thing is that those same statistics are true for couples in the church. It seems to me that one of the reasons Christians divorce at about the same rate as those who don't know Christ is that so many Christians fail to allow their faith to be an integral part of their marital relationship. When believers live their married lives with the same values, behaviors, lifestyles, and morals of their lost neighbors, it is not surprising that their marriages can easily face the same demise. There is a major difference between two Christians being married and a Christian marriage.

A Christian marriage has a foundation of faith in Christ. That means that the husband and the wife are growing toward God, both individually and as a couple. It is not a relationship made up solely of two people. Some people see marriage as a straight line between husband and wife. They spend the rest of their lives striving to draw closer to each other, only to find that the harder they try, the further apart they end up. They are like two opposite polarized magnets. You can try as hard as you can but they will never stay close together. A better view of Christian marriage is that of a triangle, including husband, wife, and God at the top. As each partner draws closer to God they automatically draw closer to each other. This spiritual aspect of marriage is essential for Christian couples:

> For married couples, spiritual meaning should be a shared pursuit. While every couple must come to an understanding of life's meaning alone, couples must also discover the meaning of their marriage together. You are not just husband and wife. You have given birth to a marriage that is very much like a living being, born from you both. And the soul of your new marriage needs nourishment. Sharing life's ultimate meaning with another person is the spiritual call of soul mates, and every couple must answer that call or risk a stunted, underdeveloped marriage. Like yeast in a loaf of bread, spirituality will ultimately determine whether your marriage rises successfully or falls disappointingly flat. The

spiritual dimension of marriage is a practical source of food for marital growth and health. No single factor does more to cultivate oneness and a meaningful sense of purpose in marriage than a shared commitment to spiritual discovery. It is the ultimate hunger of our souls.[1]

Psalm 127:1 says, "Unless the Lord builds the house, its builders labor in vain". This verse describes so many couples I know. They come to see me because their marriage is in shambles. As they tell their story they describe all the work they have invested in trying to make it better, only to feel further apart. I do not doubt their sincere efforts, but effort without the Lord's help is in vain. They need to start putting forth that same amount of effort in their growth toward God. Sometimes a couple will say, "We've tried everything," but when asked about counseling or Bible study or books on marriage or prayer, they have to admit that they really haven't tried much. If we want a godly marriage we have got to do it His way.

Jesus tells a story in Matthew 7:24-27 that illustrates the enormous difference a solid foundation can make in a person's life. He uses this story to explain the need for people to build their entire lives on Him. While this is not a passage of Scripture that's dealing specifically with the topic of marriage, the implications are obvious. The story talks about two very different foundations that can be built upon, and how that foundation determines the ultimate result.

Jesus says that it is a foolish person who builds his house on sand. The sand represents anything that doesn't last, things that are meaningless in the scope of life. How ridiculous it would be for anyone to build their dream home without first making sure that the foundation was solid and secure. Regardless of how beautiful that house may appear, the reality is that it won't last. Many people go though life thinking that what's on the outside -- the looks, the talents, the material possessions -- will sustain them for a lifetime. When times get tough, these same people realize that they are just an empty shell, a facade, and their lives begin to crumble. The same principle is true in marriage. Some couples who appear to have everything a person could ever want are the same couples whose marriages fall apart quickly and painfully when the least bit of pressure is applied. A foundation of shifting sand will never be enough to hold a person's life together or to sustain a marriage.

Several years ago while I was in California for a few weeks one of the top news stories was about a man's house that had been built on a cliff overlooking the ocean. The ground beneath this multi-million dollar home had eroded. When the news cameras showed a picture of the house I was shocked. At least one forth of it was hanging over the cliff with nothing but air beneath it! It was so dangerous that it had to be condemned, and the owner was not even allowed back inside to clear out his belongings. A portion of Pacific Coast Highway down below was temporarily shut down while this beautiful mansion was bulldozed over the cliff, crumbling into a pile of debris in the middle of the street. Sitting in my motel room that night I came to a brilliant conclusion. I would rather live in an $80,000 home on a cement slab than a multi-million dollar mansion on the edge of a cliff! (I told you it was brilliant.)

It's important to note in this passage that Jesus does not just imply that it's a bad idea to build on a foundation of sand, He says it is foolish. God is the creator and sustainer of marriage. It is this truth that draws such a harsh reaction from Christ. If God is the one who came up with the marriage concept, and He is the one who laid out all of the ground rules, and He is the source of power by which a marriage can grow, then it only follows that it would be foolish to attempt such an undertaking without Him.

While it's true that only a foolish person would attempt to build a house on a foundation of sand, Jesus says that the opposite is true of a person who builds his house on a foundation of rock. He calls this person wise. If the sand represents the temporary, unimportant, trivial things that life has to offer, then the rock must represent something of great value, something that lasts. The Scripture is abundantly clear that Jesus Christ is the Rock, the solid foundation, the only One worthy of building a life upon. King David wrote that the Lord was his Rock, and his Redeemer (Psalm 19:14). In Psalm 18:2 he says that the Lord is a fortress in whom to take refuge. The prophet Isaiah, when speaking of the Lord, described Him as the Rock eternal (Isaiah 26:4). It is this same Rock, Jesus Christ, who is to be the sure foundation of marriage. In the Matthew story, Jesus tells His listeners that His desire is for them to seek out a life built upon a solid foundation of trust in Him. This is not only true of life, but it is also true of marriage. He is to be the one who gives direction to the relationship. He brings it hope, He provides the strength, He heals the hurts, and He is the one who creates the oneness.

Another important aspect of this story is what each house must endure. The Scripture says that the storms will come, regardless of the foundation. Weather is not a respecter of houses. Wind and rain are not isolated to poor neighborhoods. Even though bad weather hits every house, the difference is seen in the type of foundation that was laid. It is the same with each individual life and with each marriage. Storms come to those who build their marriage on a solid foundation and to those who build their marriage on the sand. The only difference between the two is the amount of damage sustained and how quickly they can recover.

Being a Christian, or having a Christian marriage, does not offer immunity from hard times. At some point in life everyone has to face the death of someone they love. Money problems attack believers and non-believers alike. Sickness is not particular about who it affects, and broken relationships hurt regardless of someone's faith or lack there of. Nowhere in Scripture are believers promised that their lives will be an easy path. As a matter of fact the Bible seems to imply that for many Christians life will be extremely difficult. What the Bible does say is that when a person has a solid foundation in Jesus Christ, no matter how hard life gets, He will give the strength to get through.

The house that was built on the rock withstood the storms and stood strong. The house with a foundation of sand could not hold up under the pressure of the storm, and in the end it fell with a mighty crash. The pressure that life and society can put on a marital relationship is enormous. The winds of doubt blow, the problems rain down, and when the weather clears, only the marriages with a sound foundation will be standing. Jesus Christ wants to be that firm foundation of faith.

A Friendship to Flourish

"Is your spouse your very best friend?" That's a question my wife and I like to ask couples who attend our marriage class. It seems like an easy enough question, but you would be surprised at how difficult many people find it to answer. It's almost as if it doesn't even make sense to them that their spouse can also be their friend. Others answer in the affirmative, and yet one would be hard pressed to find any proof. Friends spend time together and hate it when they're apart. They enjoy each other's presence and laugh at each other's jokes. They work at their relationship, putting forth effort and initiative. Basically, they just like each other. I think that is a big problem with a lot of married couples. They say that they love each other, but they really don't like each other very much.

If a marriage is going to be successful husbands and wives must not only be growing closer to God, they must also be growing closer together. They have to work hard at cultivating their relationship. A destructive marriage myth says that the longer two people stay together the closer they will automatically become. Nothing could be further from the truth. The only things that will happen automatically with time is that the couple will grow old and they will also grow cold. If you don't want that to happen to your marriage there are some things you must continually do. You need to always respect, always protect, and never neglect.

Have you ever been in line at the grocery store, or sat in the bleachers at your kid's ball game, and just listened to the way other married couples talk about each other? It's embarrassing! Husbands call their wives their "old lady" or the "old ball and chain."

They complain about their nagging or about their spending habits. Wives aren't much better. When they get together in a pack they seem to feed off one another. Many describe their husbands as lazy slobs and put them down in front of their friends. When husbands and wives get together it only gets worse. They call each other names and criticize continually. They treat each other with total disrespect, and don't care if they embarrass, discourage, or crush each other's spirit. Real friends don't treat each other that way. It's enough to break your heart.

Ephesians 5:33 commands wives to respect their husbands. In the same way 1Peter 3:7 commands husbands to treat their wives with respect. I wonder what would happen when a bunch of men got together and started putting down their wives, if one man interrupted to say how much he loves the woman he married. That sure would shake things up a bit! What about if a wife started talking positively about her husband in the middle of a gripe session among her friends? I think the crowd would quiet down a little, don't you? It's amazing how far a little respect will go. If we don't respect our spouses no one else will either. But if we do show respect, it will not only strengthen our marriages, but it will encourage others to do the same.

We also need to protect our spouse, defending them with everything we've got. In the great love chapter in the Bible, I Corinthians 13, verse seven says that real love always protects. The kind of protection the Bible is talking about is physical, emotional, and verbal. It means that we stick up for each other, that we defend each other, and that we make sure no harm comes to the one we love. Physical protection seems to be a given, and may be the easiest to provide. Making sure that we don't hurt each other emotionally or verbally is more difficult to accomplish. Lovingly protecting each other from emotional pain from others is sometimes hard to do as well, especially when those others may live in our own homes. We cannot allow our children to put down or harshly criticize our spouse. They need to know that this person is our soul mate, and that no one, including them, is allowed to talk to them that way.

One day when my children were younger we went to pick them up from school. When they got in the car they told us about an incident that happened as they were awaiting their ride. My eight-year-old daughter walked up to her brother, who was ten, and began talking to him and his friends. One of the boys made a rude comment about her not being welcome in the group. My son took offense at the statement and told the other boy so. The boy got mad and said, "Do you have problem with me?", and my son said, "Yeah, I've got a big problem with you." At that, the boy turned and walked away. What a proud moment for a daddy. I commended my son on his behavior and told him that if he would continue to defend his little sister like that, he would grow up and become a great husband who knew how to defend his bride.

If we really respect each other, it makes it a whole lot easier to protect each other. If we accomplish the first two then the third should be a piece of cake. We need to make sure that we don't neglect each other. Over time, without even noticing, it is very easy to start to take each other for granted. We begin to neglect spending quality time together, staying longer hours at work, hanging out with other friends, or devoting large portions of time to our own hobbies and interests. Time is an essential element for building a solid, loving marriage. As a matter of fact, it is an essential element for building any friendship. No one has to make us spend time with our friends, it is something we want to do. Claiming that our spouse is our best friend, and yet never spending time with them, is a contradiction of terms.

The Apostle John encourages us to make sure that our love is not just words, but that it is followed up with actions that are true and meaningful (1 John 3:18). Talk is cheap, easy, and empty. Our love for each other must go deeper than just shallow words that quickly begin to loose their meaning. When it comes to friendships my wife is so much better than I am. I'll tell anyone that I have hundreds of friends. I will call someone a friend even if I haven't seen or heard from them in over twenty years! It is easy for me to point to someone in church and say, "There goes a friend of mine," and yet I have a hard time recalling their name. The reality is that I have many acquaintances, and a few good friends. Now when my wife calls you a friend you can be sure that it is so. She has a handful of great friends that she stays in touch with, spends time with, and knows what is going on in their life. She has a better understanding of the word "friend."

Our spouse is not just to be our friend, he/she is to be our best friend. It means that we have to work at the relationship, it doesn't just happen on its own. When it comes to marriage there a several things that need to be present on a regular basis if the friendship is going to grow. First, every couple needs regular, ongoing communication. Knee to knee, eye to eye, no distractions, sharing life togeth-er. While it is true that real love and friendships require more than words, words are very important. Second, every couple needs reg-ular, ongoing dating - going out and having fun together. Forgetting the bills and the kids and the jobs and the hassles of life, and just spending time together. The pressures of marriage are tremendous, and without a little relaxing time it can become overwhelming. The third thing that every couple needs on a regular, ongoing basis is prayer. Holding hands and praying out loud for each other, express-ing our love and gratitude to the Lord for each other, and asking for His strength and guidance. This is the hardest to accomplish, but it is also the most important. Statistics tell us that "only 4 percent of Christian couples actually pray together on a regular basis."[2] Those numbers are sad and prove that couple prayer is difficult to implement. Some who work with married couples have come up with their own statistics, and those numbers are staggering. Their research shows that "only one couple in 1,500 who pray together on a regular basis ever gets divorced."[3] We must understand the importance of prayer.

Next to sexual intercourse I believe that prayer is the most inti-mate activity between two people. It is bearing your soul to God in front of your spouse. Wives, hearing your husbands thank God for you and ask for His help in making them the husbands thy need to be, has got to do something for your heart. Husbands, listening as your wife tells Jesus that she loves you and wants to be the kind of wife you need, will bring you encouragement and a desire to keep working at the relationship. Couple prayer is also a good indicator of marital health. "Sociologist Andrew Greeley surveyed married people and found that the happiest couples were those who pray together. Couples who frequently pray together are twice as likely as those who pray less often to describe their marriages as being highly romantic.[4]

A Focus on Forever

The divorce statistics in America are staggering. John Gottman says that, "more than half of all first marriages end in divorce. Second marriages do worse, failing at a rate of about 60 percent."[5] These statistics are not only disheartening, they are also displeasing to the Lord. God's Word tells us in Malachi 2:13-16 that God hates divorce. Not only does this passage allow us a glimpse into God's heart on this issue, it also clearly lays out the reasons for His strong command. God hates divorce because it is the breaking of a covenant made between two people on their wedding day. A second reason God despises divorce is that it destroys the oneness that He desires for every couple. Children are a key issue when it comes to ending a marriage, and it breaks God's heart to see them hurting. Finally, one major aspect of divorce that is seldom recognized is the way that it affects each person's relationship with God.

When a couple stands before the Lord on their wedding day and pledge vows to each other, God takes it seriously. The problem is, many of those same couples do not have the same level of intensity or loyalty. Making an oath to God, or to another person in the presence of God, is a very serious matter. The oath is binding and the commitment is to be fulfilled. O. Palmer Robertson, in his book, The Christ of the Covenants, says, "This closeness of relationship between oath and covenant emphasizes that a covenant in its essence is a bond. By the covenant, persons become committed to one another."[6] Therefore, breaking this kind of covenant is not something that the Lord takes lightly, nor should those who made it. God says that He is displeased with divorce, because the husband is breaking faith with the wife of his marriage covenant.

Divorce was not a part of God's plan for mankind. He intended for one man and one woman to be together for a lifetime. Jesus made this clear when the Pharisees were trying to corner Him on this issue. They recalled Moses' allowance for divorce, and asked Christ to explain this provision. Jesus states that Moses permitted divorce only because of the hardness of man's heart. He also removes any doubt as to where God's heart is on the matter of divorce when He says that "it was not this way from the beginning" (Matthew 19:3-8). God sees the marriage covenant as a binding agreement between husband and wife that is not to be broken until death.

A second reason why God hates divorce is based on His desire for each couple to find oneness. In the Malachi passage God says that He has made each couple one. Jesus echoes this when He says that a man shall leave his parents and be united to his wife, thus becoming one flesh. And because it was God who joined them together, man should not separate them. This was Jesus' response in Matthew 19:5-6 to the question from the Pharisees as to whether divorce should be permitted. This oneness, this closeness, this unity is God's desire for every married couple, and He hates watching it be destroyed by divorce.

Another reason divorce breaks God's heart is because of the way it affects the children. Scripture is clear about God's heart for children as is shown in Matthew 18:2-6 when Jesus says He loves for little ones to be around Him. He says that no one can enter the kingdom of heaven unless they come as a child. He states that anyone who welcomes a child is welcoming Him, and He also issues a strong warning for anyone who harms a child. Later on He rebukes the disciples for not allowing small children to come to Him (Matthew 19:13,14).

"Divorce is often a war between fathers and mothers. Tragically, children can become the orphans of that war."[7] This is an accurate, and yet sad picture of the truth. In the aforementioned Malachi passage, God says that when a divorce takes place it has a direct impact on the kids. He challenges husbands not to break faith with their wives because He desires godly offspring. God obviously sees a connection between divorce and the spiritual health of the children. This passage is not saying that godly kids cannot come from broken homes, but it does imply that it is much more difficult.

Finally, God hates divorce because of the adverse affect it has on that couple's relationship with Him. This passage says that many times the reason God does not hear prayers or accept offerings is because of the issue of divorce. This hard-hearted response to marital difficulties sets up barriers in the spiritual realm. This thought is repeated by Peter when he says that if husbands do not treat their wives with consideration and respect it could lead to their prayers being hindered (1 Peter 3:7). If the way a husband and wife treat each other during their marriage can have such an adverse affect on their walk with God, then certainly divorce could have a major impact on their spiritual lives.

God says that He hates divorce. If God says He hates something, but we still see it as a viable option, we need to check our relationship with Him. We all know that the Bible makes a few exceptions to the no divorce clause, but even those do not change God's hatred for the dissolution of marriage. He does give us an opportunity to end a marriage where adultery has taken place, but just because He allows it does not mean that is His desire. With God's help I believe that almost every marriage can make it.

Commitment in marriage is to continue until broken by death. That is the promise we made when we stood before the Lord and pledged our love to each other. It was not just a quaint idea, or a heartfelt desire, or a matter of marriage procedure - it was a promise, a vow. This promise said that we would stay for better or for worse, in sickness and in health, for richer or for poorer, until separated by death. We need to take those words very seriously. It is a matter of loyalty. It is also a matter of integrity. Half of the people who say those words later prove that they really didn't mean them. Nobody ever said it was going to be easy, because it won't be. But every one of us who got married said that we would stick it out, no matter what. That is a focus on forever.

When the preacher asks, "for better or for worse," it is not an either/or question. We cannot stand up and respond, "for better!" It is a both/and question. Are we willing to commit the rest of our lives to this person whether things get better or whether they get worse? That is the question. Most people respond, "we do," even though around half of the couples in the United States really don't. It appears that what many couples are committing themselves to is "till divorce do us part." Divorce has become acceptable, even expected. When talking about their marriage problems many people will say to me, "John, this is not what I bargained for." Then I have to look them dead in the eyes and tell them that this is exactly what they bargained for! The commitment they made did not just say, "do you take this person for better, in health, and richer." And yet that seems like the only part they really meant.

What every couple needs to learn to do is shut the divorce door. Imagine sitting in your office with a full days worth of work to do. The office is a little stuffy, so you open the door and prop it open, giving you a great view outside. As you get back to work you feel the cool breeze blowing, you hear the birds singing and the children playing, and the sunshine casts a glare on your computer screen. How long do you think you will be able to concentrate on your work? How long will it be before you give up trying and go outside to enjoy the fresh air? The constant thought that "out there" is going to be so much better than "in here" will ultimately pull you away, and your work will never be finished. That is a picture of too many marriages these days. They are leaving the divorce door wide open, always acknowledging it as an option if things don't work out. They say they are committed to making it work, but every time things get tough they begin to look out the door. It looks so much better out there. As long as the divorce door is open the couple has two options. They can do the hard work it takes to make their marriage succeed, or they can walk out the door. I believe that if they don't shut that door they will ultimately walk through it. When the door is slammed shut and boarded over they are also left with two options. They can do the hard work to make their marriage succeed, or they can keep living in it the way it is. I have found that when those are the two options, more couples are willing to do whatever it takes to make it work. Neither of them wants to continue in their pain and dysfunction.

Proverbs 18:22 says that the man who finds a wife finds a good thing. I believe that the same could be said for a woman who finds a husband. Marriage is a good thing. It is definitely worth committing to and working to make better.

Chapter 2

COMPATIBILITY

Not long ago I heard an advertisement on the radio for a dating service that guaranteed each person who paid for their services that they could find them a match that was 95% compatible. Their slogan was as follows "Call today, meet someone tomorrow." Wouldn't it be great if it was that easy? A simple phone call, a completed questionnaire, a picture or two, and voila, a match made in heaven. Real life and the current divorce statistics tell us that it is much more difficult than it seems. In a book called Gender and Grace, the authors make a powerful statement about the gaping differences between men and women, and how hard compatibility is to find. "Created social and sexual, we sense that we cannot live without each other. Fallen, and carrying the burden of Genesis 3:16, we too often find that we cannot live peaceably with each other either."[1] In other words, "Can't live with 'em, can't live without 'em." In this chapter we will be addressing several key differences between the sexes that make genuine compatibility difficult. When all of these areas are combined it is a wonder any marriage is successful.

Gender Differences

The biggest difference between a man and a woman is that one is a man and the other is a woman! Genesis 1:27 says, "So God created man in His own image, in the image of God He created him; male and female He created them." Men and women were created to be different, but with the capability of enjoying oneness. The fall did not destroy that possibility, but it made it much more difficult. Once sin entered the picture compatibility became even harder to achieve. It can be illustrated in a joke I once heard. Adam was looking very sad, so God asked him what was wrong. Adam said he didn't have anyone to talk to. God told Adam that He would give him a companion, and it would be a woman. He said, "This person will cook for you and wash your clothes, she will always agree with every decision you make. She will bear your children and never ask you to get up in the middle of the night to take care of them. She will not nag you and will always be the first to admit she was wrong when you've had a disagreement. She will never have a headache and will freely give you love and passion whenever you need it." Adam asked God, "What will a woman like this cost?" "An arm and a leg," God replied. Adam asked, "What can I get for just a rib?" And the rest is history.

There are several different aspects to gender differences. The first is the mental aspect. In general, men and women think and process thoughts differently. Most men focus on their accomplishments, while most women focus on their relationships. It comes natural for a man to find his self-worth in his work, what he does. Whereas most women find their self-worth in their family, who they are. When a man hears his wife share a problem he usually wants to solve it. When a woman shares a problem with her husband she usually wants him to understand her feelings. A major difference is seen in the way most men and women listen. If I answer the phone when it rings at my house, and hear some good friends tell me about the birth of their new baby, several key elements may get lost in translation. My wife can easily get frustrated with me after a few probing questions. "Was it a boy or a girl? How much did it weigh? How long was it? Was the mom in labor for a long time? How are mom and baby doing? What is the little one's name?" My only response will be "They had a baby!" I guarantee if my wife answered the phone she would know the answer to every one of those questions by the time she hung up. The truth is that most men listen for the main point, while most women listen for the details. These mental differences can become extremely irritating.

The second key gender difference involves the **emotional** aspect. In his best selling book, *His Needs / Her Needs*,[2] Willard Harley clearly lays out the basic needs of the average man and woman. Take a look at what his research found to be the top five needs of a woman and the top five needs of a man.

HIS NEEDS	HER NEEDS
Sexual Fulfillment	Affection
Recreational Companionship	Conversation
An Attractive Spouse	Honesty & Openness
Domestic Support	Financial Support
Admiration	Family Commitment

Harley says that the average man wants his wife to pat him on the back and boost his ego, go hunting and golfing with him, keep the house nice and tidy, maintain her youthful beauty, and be ready to jump in the sack at the drop of a hat. The average woman looks to her husband for comfort and cuddling, hours of meaningful conversation, the promise that family comes first, telling her the truth, the whole truth, and bringing home a nice paycheck on the first and the fifteenth. Does anyone see how this might lead to problems? John Barry, the humor columnist, summed it up in this statement. "What do women want? Women want to be loved, to be listened to, to be desired, to be respected, to be needed, to be trusted, and sometimes, just to be held. What do men want? Tickets to the World Series!"

The third key gender difference is the **physical** aspect. I picked up my son from school one day when he was about nine-years-old. On the back seat of my car was a book I had been reading on gender differences. When my son saw the book he said, "I know all about gender differences, we learned that in school. Men have a penis and women have phalanges." Trying not to laugh I said, "Well, that is true, but I don't think that is the word you were looking for." After a brief discussion he remembered the right word, and we continued a very interesting talk about the differences between the sexes.

Everyone knows about the obvious differences in the human anatomy, and we are grateful for them, but that is not the only physical difference. Body changes that take place over the years can add to the difficulty in finding compatibility. Women go through hormonal changes, they suffer through their menstrual cycle, they experience the changes associated with pregnancy, and they ultimately face menopause. Both men and women must deal with these changes appropriately. Women need to act with responsibility, not blaming every bad mood or irritable action on PMS. Men need to act lovingly, with understanding and sympathy, being patient with their wives and what they have to go through.

I am always amazed when I hear people justify living together before marriage based on the issue of anatomical differences. The old, "you wouldn't buy a pair of shoes before you try them on, would you?" argument doesn't hold water. The most compatible aspect of our gender differences is our anatomy. God made us, male and female, and amazingly we fit! Our physical attributes are very compatible, but our physical desires aren't. Facts prove that pre-marital sex and living together only complicate the issue, and result in more failed marriages. The gender issues that make compatibility so difficult to achieve have more to do with who we are than how we look. Mentally, emotionally, and physically we are as different as night and day, and we need the Lord's help to make it all work out.

Personality Differences

Isn't it funny how the very things that draw us together in the first place, can later on end up pushing us apart? It does seem true that before marriage opposites attract, and after marriage opposites attack. I love listening to couples complain about their spouse's personality flaws only to turn around and say that those very same issues were what attracted them to each other in the first place. One woman will say about her husband, "He never says a word. I can't get him to communicate with me. He just sits there like a bump on a log, and never opens his mouth. It drives me crazy." When I ask her what it was about this man that she was initially attracted to, she will say, "He was the strong, silent type. I just loved that in him." Another wife will complain about her husband never being serious, always joking around, being loud and obnoxious. When I ask her what she found attractive about him early on, she will say, "I loved his sense of humor!" How quickly that cute little voice becomes annoying. It doesn't take long before that strong leadership quality turns into a control freak. At first he loved the fact that she always spoke her mind, but now she has become a complaining nag. Be careful what you ask for, you just might get it.

Over many years of doing marriage counseling I have found that this is the number one detriment to genuine compatibility. Our personality is who we are, how we act, what we think, and how we treat each other. Our personalities are ingrained in us, and they are not easy to change. Granted, we all have personality flaws that we need to correct, but no one should ever ask us to change who we are. Therefore we all need to take our time during the dating period and make sure that this person, flaws and all, is who we want to spend the rest of our lives with. A major key when it comes to compatibility in the area of personality differences is acceptance. We need to learn to accept our spouse for who they are, and not try to change them to become who we want them to be.

Several years ago my wife and I attended a counseling conference where one of my favorite professors, Dr. Arch Hart, spoke on this topic. He told a story about his own marriage, about how different he and his wife are. He said that over the years he had worked hard at trying to accept her personality, not allowing it to frustrate him. One day, while he was watching her minister to another young lady, the Holy Spirit convicted him that he was not supposed to just accept her the way she is, he was supposed to celebrate her and the wonderful way God had made her. That little talk had a major impact on our marriage. Accepting each other's differences implies that we are just learning to put up with them, in spite of the fact that they still drives us crazy. Celebrating each other's differences includes thanking God for them, understanding that they were uniquely created the way that God wanted them, and that He has brought them into our life to enrich us.

It is important for all of us to understand our own personality type, strengths and weaknesses, and to understand how it fits with the personality type of our spouse. There are many different inventories and tests available to help us in this quest. It really doesn't matter if they talk about letters of the alphabet or breeds of dogs, the important thing is that they help us see ourselves clearer. The personality inventory that I am most familiar with is Mels Carbonel's, *Uniquely You.*[3] He uses the DISC personality model.

The "D" type personality, or the choleric, is outgoing and task oriented. Their main characteristics are that they are dominant, demanding, and decisive. They are doers who are very driven to succeed. Just give them a challenging task and sit back and watch them go. No task is too big or too challenging. These people are natural leaders with strong personalities. Others naturally follow D types. Along with these obvious strengths come some areas to concentrate on. Cholerics need to work at being gentle, acknowledging their tendency toward bossiness and control A good Scripture verse for the D type personality is James 3:17. "But the wisdom that comes from heaven is first of all pure; then peace-loving, considerate, submissive, full of mercy and good fruit, impartial and sincere."

The "I" type personality, or the sanguine, is also outgoing, but they are more people oriented. These type people are interactive, influencing, and impressive. They are the life of the party, fun to be around, liked by most. Most I type people have never met a stranger. Fifteen minutes after walking into a room all the attention is focused on them. While there are many strengths to this personality type, here again there is room for improvement. Sanguines can easily dominate a conversation, not allowing anyone else a chance to speak. They need to work on their listening skills, realizing that they don't always have to be the one talking. God's Word has something to say to the I type personality in James 1:19. "My dear brothers, take note of this: Everyone should be quick to listen, slow to speak and slow to become angry."

The "S" type personality, or phlegmatic, is people oriented, but they are more reserved. They are characterized by steadiness, submissiveness, stability, and security. S types are easy going and relaxed. They don't easily get their feathers ruffled, and they demonstrate consistency and concern. Phlegmatics make good workers as well as good friends. They are more "behind the scenes" people, who don't look for much recognition. Along with these character strengths come a few glaring weaknesses. This type of personality, because they are so submissive and steady, can allow others to run all over them. They seldom speak up for themselves, and they can easily become worriers. A good verse for phlegmatics to learn is Joshua 1:6, "Be strong and courageous, because you will lead these people to inherit the land I swore to their forefathers to give them."

The "C" type personality, or melancholy, is task oriented and reserved. They can be characterized as cautious, calculating, competent, critical, and compliant. Melancholies are very organized and meticulous. They will never jump into a situation or task without first giving it serious attention. Their thought processes are always activated, and they approach each new project with caution and planning. The negative aspects of the melancholy personality include their critical nature, condemning tendencies, and overly cautious behavior. Their attention to detail can sometimes cause them to miss the big picture. A good Scripture verse for the C type person is I Thessalonians 4:18, "Therefore encourage each other with these words."

Each marriage is made up of these contrasting personality styles. The extreme differences can lead to all kinds of barriers to compatibility. Even if two people with the same personality type marry, problems can arise. These two may be too much alike, driving each other crazy with their similarities. Knowing that God created us the way we are, and that He brought us together, allows us to trust that He will help us work through our personality differences. Each person brings to the table strengths that their partner needs and can benefit from, as well as weaknesses that their partner can pray for and help correct. There is a line in the movie "Rocky" that illustrates this point. When speaking of his wife, Adrienne, Rocky makes this brilliant deduction: "I got gaps and she's got gaps, but together we ain't got no gaps." Beautiful!

Role Differences

Everyone comes into marriage with their own pre-conceived ideas of what it should be like. Over the years we have developed our own concepts of what roles the husband should play and what roles the wife should occupy. The Word of God has given us a clear picture of what the relationship between husband and wife should be like. The Apostle Paul tells us in Ephesians 5 that the wife is to submit to her husband as unto the Lord, and that the husband is to love his wife as Christ loved the church. I really believe that if we could just live out these two verses all the rest would take care of itself. The problem is that we like to read each other's mail.

Most men love that verse about a wife submitting to her husband, and they enjoy reminding her of that responsibility regularly. Most women cling to the verse that says a husband should love his wife with a Christ-like love, and whenever possible they throw that up in their husband's face. Men need to understand that verse 22 was not written for their benefit. That verse comes straight from the heart of God to His daughters. He is lovingly showing them their part in a beautiful marriage. We can skip right over that verse, but we don't skip down too much, because we need to camp out on verse 25. Ladies must realize that verse 25 is not for them. God wrote this challenge to his sons, offering them loving guidance to help them make their marriages what He wants them to be. If we would just spend our time concentrating on the verse that was written to us, and stop worrying about whether or not our spouse is adhering to their verse, we would be much happier and much more successful.

One of my favorite authors is Larry Crabb. When talking about the issue of compatibility as it relates to these verses he says the following:

> Many husbands pervert Paul's teaching on headship into a warrant for requiring their wives to always agree with them and to service their every need. Others, attempting to correct this mistake, have renounced any distinctive masculine form of loving their wives and have watched their marriage shift from a cold regime with a leader and a follower into a business arrangement marked more by efficiency than intimate passion. And countless wives respond to the confusion either by submitting themselves into the status of a kept woman or a domestic servant, losing all sense of personal dignity, or by liberating themselves into a larger world where they enjoy the respect they deserve while silently crying for the love they want.[4]

Everyone comes into marriage with **High Expectations**, and that is not necessarily a bad thing. Problems arise when our expectations are diametrically opposed to each other. My wife grew up in a home where both parents worked. That meant that everyone pitched in with the household chores, helping out with the yard work as well as with cooking and cleaning. I grew up more "Leave It To Beaver." My Dad worked outside the home while my Mom stayed home and took care of the house and kids. For some strange reason we never gave this much thought before we got married, just assuming everything would fall into place. Well, it didn't quite work out that smoothly. Our first full week together in our new life found me going to school full-time and Pamela working full-time. About 6:00 one evening we found ourselves standing in the kitchen looking at each other with the same question on our minds, "What's for dinner?" It didn't take long before we realized that we needed a clear plan, because our expectations were not being met.

Simple things like who washes the clothes and cooks, and who mows the lawn and maintains the car, can be a source of contention. While society seems to make clear distinctions between what is "man's work" and what is "woman's work," that doesn't always play itself out with each couple. As chauvinistic as I was when we got married, I had to make some major adjustments. I never learned how to work on cars growing up. My dad didn't know much about it, and he was kind enough to pass on his lack of knowledge to me. My wife, on the other hand, grew up with a daddy who knew everything about automobile maintenance. I'll never forget the first day I realized that something seemed odd about our relationship. I had been inside cleaning up and cooking dinner while my wife was outside in the yard and tinkering with the car. I stuck my head out the front door and called out for her to come on inside and wash up, because it was time to eat. I stood there stunned thinking, "something's not right with this picture!"

Expectations can easily turn into misconceptions. The following is a list of what I call "Marriage Mythconceptions." They are statements many of us believe to be fact, when in reality there is very little truth to them. Buying into these untruths can damage our relationships.

Marriage Mythconceptions

1) <u>Marriage partners should have a lot in common, and enjoy most of the same things.</u>

While it is true that husbands and wives need to find some common interests, it is not true that we have to share all of our likes and dislikes. Variety is the spice of life and opposites attract. Early in our marriage we went to a marriage conference. The speaker encouraged each couple to take an interest in their partner's hobbies. We decided to give it a try. Saturday morning rolled around and I got up early to accompany Pamela to the mall. It was great, for the first 45 minutes. After that I began to grow tired of walking around the same dress rack over and over and over! My feet started hurting, I was getting hungry, and there was no place to sit down. Our quality time together quickly turned into a heated discussion about how much time is really needed to pick out one dress. Thankfully, we finally made it home. Now it was my turn. Pamela agreed to sit with me and watch an entire ball game. It was great, for about the first 20 minutes. My wife didn't seemed to understand that watching a ball game included listening to the play by play. She thought it would be a great time for conversation. I disagreed. We were crushed by our failed attempt at learning to enjoy what the other enjoyed. We abandoned the advice of the conference speaker and decided on a new plan. I would watch sports while Pamela went to the mall, then we would go out to eat together afterwards and discuss the events of the day. What a blissful arrangement!

2) <u>My spouse will make me whole.</u>

Too many people who are miserable being single think that getting married will bring the ultimate happiness. The idea is that two incomplete people can come together and make one complete relationship. That is a faulty concept. The truth is that two 50% people make for a 50% marriage! If we are not fulfilled, content, and satisfied in our single life we will not find that fulfillment in marriage. It is one thing to have a heart-felt longing to get married. It is another to believe that without a spouse we will never be a whole person.

3) <u>If we have a Christian marriage we will never have major problems.</u>

This kind of thinking has been around for years, and is a favorite teaching of some television evangelists. The idea is that once you give your heart and life to Jesus you will never face hard times again. All Christians, and of course, all Christian marriages, are immune from hard times, bad days, or even Satan's attacks. Nothing could be further from the truth. As a matter of fact, the Bible says that Christians are one of the devil's main targets. He loves to harass, threaten, deceive, discourage, and torment those who belong to the Lord. He knows he has lost the overall war, but he loves to keep fighting the little battles. A husband and wife who love the Lord, and are even building their whole life and marriage on Him and His Word, are still not immune to problems. We must remember the Lord said that storms come to those who build on the rock as well as the sand.

4) <u>If we are really in love, we will agree on most everything.</u>

Once again here is the notion that love conquers all. We may have totally different personalities, families of origin, and political persuasions, but if we are in love, all of those things will blend perfectly together. Therefore, if we disagree or argue, we must not real-ly be in love. This mythconception is often complicated by the fact that during the dating phase these differences did not arise. That period of mental fog called engagement convinces us that we see everything the same way. We must be meant for each other. How-ever, when the fog clears into the reality of marriage, and the dis-agreements begin to raise their ugly heads, then we are sure that we have been deceived. Our partner must have lied to us all along, just to trick us into marriage. And now we are stuck with someone who is completely incompatible. This certainly can't be love, can it?

5) <u>If this is the person God has for me, he/she will fulfill all my dreams and expectations.</u>

The problem here is that we all enter marriage with warped dreams and expectations. We all had ideas, that we got from who knows where, and those ideas are far from reality. I am con-vinced that the two most destructive publications that have ever been written were Playboy Magazine and Romance Novels. Many young men and women grow up reading this trash and develop their ideas as to what marriage should be for them. Many men go into the marriage assuming that their new bride will always look fit, will always desire sex, wherever, whenever, and however they want it, and that their wife's sex drive is every bit as strong as their own. It doesn't take long before they are feeling let down, confused, and wronged, thinking that they got a raw deal. It is not uncommon for a woman to enter this new matrimonial state believing that her husband will woo her with flowers and candies and love poems on a regular basis. She is sure that he will be constantly dreaming up different ways to sweep her off her feet and carry her into new romantic adventures. Quickly she begins to realize the truth, and cannot help but feel disappointment and frustration over how she has been done wrong. And now they are faced with a lifetime together filled with hurt, frustrations, and unfulfilled dreams.

6) <u>If we are really in love, we will automatically know what the other wants and needs.</u>

In this mythconception real love equates to mind reading. If my spouse really loves me he/she will know what I am thinking and will act on that knowledge. If they don't, it is because they just don't care. And when they claim ignorance it is seen as an excuse, an intentional attempt at covering up for their insensitivity. Therefore, when I need a hug, my spouse should sense that, and come hold me. When I just want her to listen, she should know that, and quietly hear me out. When she is upset with me, I should be so closely connected to her that I know without a doubt what is bothering her. This kind of thinking values assumptions over communication. While it may be easier to assume I know what is on my wife's mind, it is much more productive if I ask her. Openly and honestly sharing our needs, wants, and hurts, allows our spouse the opportunity to respond in a healthy manner, without pressuring them to be the Amazing Kreskin.

7) <u>If we have a good sex life, then we have a good marriage.</u>

Sex is an important aspect of the marital relationship, but it is not the most important one. A couple can be very compatible sexually, while still struggling in several other areas of their marriage. I have been amazed over the years at couples who are even separated because of their vast differences, but who will still get together regularly for sex! They tell me that while they have no desire to live with each other right now, they still enjoy getting their physical needs met by their spouse. Other couples on the verge of divorce have shared with me that their sex life was not part of the problem, but all the other issues were just too massive for them to overcome. Struggling in the sexual arena does not constitute the end of a marriage, and a healthy sex life does not guarantee marital success.

8) <u>Intimacy and love automatically increase throughout the years of marriage.</u>

This mindset believes that love and closeness are a natural by-product of time. Actually, the exact opposite is true. Left on their own, with no thought or effort, love and intimacy will fade and ultimately disintegrate. Growing love and intimacy takes time, hard work, prayer, and determination. It is a process that includes struggle and disappointment. I remember when Pamela and I first got married. I thought she was going into it wearing rose colored glasses. I felt I had a much more mature view of marriage. I knew that it was going to be tough, and that everything was not going to be a romantic love story. Being older than Pamela, I tried to share with her my years of wisdom and perspective. In reality, my ideas were immature and unrealistic. Although I did have some understanding of how hard marriage was going to be, my mind kept telling me that after a certain numbers of years everything would get easier. I truly believed that after a decade or so, we would settle in to this comfortable relationship that needed very little effort. That day hasn't arrived yet. I'm beginning to believe it never will.

9) <u>Everything good in our relationship will get better.</u>

If we communicate well now, we will get better and better at it as the years go by. If we handle conflict in a constructive manner now, we will never struggle with it in the future. If our sex life is fulfilling, it will always be fulfilling. What is good now will be great down the road. There is no chance that things could turn south. That will never happen to us. Those are the words of the eternal optimist couple beginning their life together. Again, there is the idea that when left on their own things progress. The problem is that is contrary to the 2nd Law of Thermodynamics, which states that things, when left to themselves, will progressively get worse. The only way life will get better and better is if much time and effort are poured into it.

10) <u>Everything bad in our relationship will go away.</u>

This is similar to number nine. This mythconception says that if we just turn a blind eye and a deaf ear to the problems in our relationship, over time they will completely disappear. How many engaged women justify marrying their easily angered fiancé because they just know that with time he will grow out of his hostile behavior? How many young men convince themselves that after marriage their new bride will mature and no longer handle financial matters irresponsibly? Their reasoning is that true love will erase poor choices and improper behavior. With time they will realize they were mistaken.

Not only can high expectations lead to marital struggles, but so can our home examples. All of us grew up with examples of what a husband and wife should be like. Some of those examples were good and some were not. We watched our mom and developed ideas as to what a wife should be. Our dads molded our image of the husband's role. Those ideas are ingrained is us from an early age. Some of us grew up with a stay at home mom and a dad who worked long, hard hours. Others watched both their parents drive off to work each day, and came home from school each afternoon alone. Some grew up in a single parent home, watching one person play the role of mom and dad. Some had the privilege of being raised in a Christian home, while church and religion were foreign concepts to many. Some kids experienced love, acceptance, encouragement and support from their parents. For others the thought of dad coming home from work struck fear into their hearts. Marital strife and conflict filled some of our homes, while others saw mom and dad acting loving and affectionate toward each other. We bring these images into our own marriages, whether we want to or not.

If we are not careful we can find ourselves saying things like, "That's not the way my mom did it," or "My dad always handled that for my mom." We can draw comparisons that are unhealthy and unhelpful. Everything from cooking and cleaning to working on the car and paying the bills can become a source of conflict. A healthy marriage learns to evaluate their family of origin's strengths and weaknesses. Then they can keep what worked and discard everything else.

When it comes to many of our differences we really don't want to change. One big hindrance to genuine compatibility is the huge excuses we make. We are very different, and there are many valid reasons why that is so. But, sometimes we like staying the way we are, refusing to put any effort into making changes that would be helpful to our relationship. Instead of working on our weaknesses we justify them. Instead of trying to make our marriage better, we settle for mediocrity, blaming our past or our parents for our short-comings. We say things like, "Why can't you accept me the way I am?" or "This is the way God made me," or even "You knew I was like this when you married me." It is basically a weak attempt to place all of the responsibility for our marital differences on someone else's shoulders. When it comes to role expectations we can't allow someone to force us into a role we're not comfortable with, but we also can't be so rigid that we refuse to change for the good of the relationship.

Gender, personality, and role differences play a major part in marital compatibility. When a man and a woman with extremely different personalities and completely opposite expectations marry and stay that way for a lifetime it is nothing short of a miracle. That is why every couple needs to give their personalities, faults and all, to the Lord. Only He can make such differences strengths instead of weaknesses.

Chapter 3

COMMUNICATION

Most every marital problem finds it's root in communication. It doesn't matter if the problem is finances, children, conflict, in-laws or sex, the real issue is communication. If a couple can talk to each other, then each of these issues can be worked out. If they can't, then each of these issues become major stumbling blocks. Learning how to share feelings and desires, and how to listen to each other's heart, is a difficult process. There are several aspects of communication that must be mastered.

Learning to Express

We all express ourselves in two ways; verbal and non-verbal. We are familiar with the phrase, "actions speak louder than words." And while that may be true, words are extremely important. The interesting thing about communication is that two people can use the exact same words, but mean something entirely different by them. My wife and I have experienced this over the years. Take the word "intimate" for example. When my wife says that we need more intimate time together she could be saying that she wants some quiet, alone time with me, so that we can talk and draw closer to each other. If I tell Pamela that I want some intimate time with

her I could mean that I want more physical touch and sexual closeness. If I come home from work and hear the words, "let's talk," it
could cause me to drop my head and sigh, assuming that I am in
trouble and in for a long lecture. In reality, Pamela may just desire
some of my undivided attention so that she can share some things
that are on her heart. And how about the phrase, "I need to stop by
Walmart for a minute." I am convinced that my "minute" and her
"minute" don't mean the same thing.

Body language is also a big way we express ourselves. It is not
very difficult for me to know what my wife is feeling just by looking at her. Her posture, the way she looks at me, and her facial
expressions, all give me a good indication of what is going on inside
her. Anger, fear, frustration, boredom, confusion, and impatience,
are all easily identifiable, based solely on expression. We must be
careful when trying to communicate with our spouse that we don't
allow our body language to cancel out what we are trying to say.

We must learn how to express **Openly**. Communication between a husband and a wife needs to be clear and specific. It is
easy to get into the habit of beating around the bush, instead of
saying what you mean and meaning what you say. We don't need
to play games, trying to make our spouse guess what is really on
our mind. Those kinds of games lead to assumptions, which can kill
a relationship. One of the keys to healthy communication is testing
every assumption verbally. If you are not sure what your spouse is
trying to say, or if you are confused by his/her actions, ask. Many
arguments can be avoided just by a little clarification. Develop the
habit of being honest with your feelings, and allowing your spouse

to be honest with theirs. We must be careful to listen and accept our partner's feelings when we ask for them.

There are several blocks to openness in communication. The first block is fear. It is easy for me to ask my wife to share her feelings, promising her that I want to know what is on her mind and heart, and then turn around and condemn her for what she shares. If this happens a few times she will be afraid to open up to me for fear of being put down, ridiculed, corrected, or rejected. If I am going to ask her to share openly and honestly with me I must also be willing to listen to her with open ears and an open mind. If I don't, she will slowly begin to shut down emotionally and close me off from her deepest feelings. Ultimately our relationship will become nothing more than surface communication.

A second block to openness is distractions. It is difficult to share heart to heart without undivided attention. Television, children, sickness, work, and family schedules can all be detrimental to meaningful conversation. Couples need knee-to-knee, eye-to-eye, focused attention in order to open up to each other. It is easy to allow life to interfere with love. If enough time goes by without intimate conversation, the relationship will begin to suffer.

Martin Seligman describes the third block to openness in what he coined "learned helplessness."[1] His research shows that people are quick to give up after they have failed a few times. The mentality is, "I have tried this in the past and it has never worked, so why should I think it will work now?" Past failures extinguish future effort. Therefore, a husband and wife who have tried to have open and honest communication in the past, only to crash and burn in their efforts, are less likely to try again. They become gun shy, admitting defeat in advance, basically quitting before they ever even get started.

Learning to express openly is only part of the equation. We must also learn to express ourselves **Lovingly**. Openness without love can be painful. People always perceive the truth without love as an attack. We need to learn to speak to each other like we love each other. A good question to ask is, "would I talk to my best friend this way?" Many times we use words, attitudes, and a tone of voice with our spouse that we would never dream of using with a friend. Loving communication uses "I" statements in place of "you" statements. We all get our backs up when others come at us with accusing words and pointing fingers.

We need to ask a few questions before we share what's on our mind. The first question: "Is it true?" The Bible says that we are to "speak the truth in love." Even hurtful words can be accepted if they are truthful and shared in a spirit of love. It is important to check our sources and verify the facts before we say things that may not be true. Many relationships have suffered irreparable damage because of false accusations and lying tongues. The second question: "Is it necessary?" The fact that it is true does not mean that it should be shared. Some things are better off when kept to ourselves. We have to check our motives. Am I wanting to share this for their benefit or for my own? The third question: "Is it helpful?" Will my husband/wife be better off because I shared this with them? It may be true, and I may even feel like it is a necessity, but if I honestly believe that my spouse will not be helped in any way by what I have to say, then I probably should keep it to myself.

Communicating lovingly does not mean that we never discuss things that bother us. A few years ago I was reading a book by John Gottman when I came across a statement that caught me off guard. I had to read it several times before I understood what he was trying to say, and I had to read it several more times before I decided that I agreed with his point. He says that complaining is one of the healthiest activities in a marriage![2] That sounds so contrary to my own experience. Pamela nor I seem to enjoy it very much when the other is complaining. But, read his statement again. He doesn't say that complaining is one of the most enjoyable activities in a marriage, he says it is one of the healthiest. He says that living in a marriage where no one is allowed to voice their complaints is like living in a jail. There is freedom in sharing what is on your mind, even if what is on your mind is negative. He goes on to say that one of the most destructive activities in a marriage is criticism. The distinction is that while it is healthy to voice complaints about situations that you wish would change, it is detrimental to a relationship to attack someone's character by criticizing who they are. Again, one addresses a behavior, while the other attacks the person. One can be done in love, while the other cannot.

Another way we need to learn to express ourselves is **Patiently**. Sometimes the hardest person to be patient with is our spouse. Ephesians 4:2 says that we are to "be patient, bearing with one another in love." Isn't it amazing how that seems to be easier to do with every other person than it is with our spouse? For some reason those we love the most can also frustrate us the most. For that reason patience is a virtue that is desperately needed within the bonds of matrimony.

We must bear with each other as we are striving to learn better communication patterns. Breaking old habits and learning new ones takes time. Impatience and irritability is a sign of poor communication and will ultimately cause our spouse to shut down, having little or no desire to even try and talk with us any more. Over time our spouses learn to become helpless in communication, and we have been their teachers. With effort and prayer we can change the momentum. The key to conquering impatience in marriage is empathy. We need to develop the art of seeing every situation through each other's eyes. I read a statement somewhere that said 90% of marriage problems can be worked through if we will just see things through the eyes of our spouse. I believe that is probably true. Genuine understanding goes a long way toward restoring healthy communication. It breaks down walls and restores trust, as we learn to express openly, lovingly, and patiently.

Learning to Esteem

Empathy is seeing things through each other's eyes. Esteem is seeing each other as more important than yourself. Proverbs 22:1 says that being esteemed is better than silver or gold. It is a precious treasure when your spouse puts your needs ahead of his/her own. The problem lies in the fact that esteeming other's needs as higher than our own is in reality an extremely difficult thing to do. We need the Lord's help to accomplish this goal.

Learning to esteem means that the # **1 Person** in my life is my spouse. I must spend my time trying to understand what she is feeling, and considering those feelings more important to me than my own. When my wife hurts, I hurt for her and with her. My life, my energy, my time, and my love need to be poured into her. When decisions need to be made, I should always consult her, and value her opinion. In every situation I should try to put myself in her shoes (even though I don't look good in heals), and try to understand what she is thinking. From my perspective, the most important person in my marriage has by far got to be my wife.

Putting our spouse first is a good goal, but there is a catch. The first thing I tell many couples when they come to see me is that I already know their main problem, even before they share one story. It's easy, because their #1 **Problem** is your #1 Problem and my #1 Problem: selfishness. It is very hard for us to let our spouse be #1 in our marriage when we are already occupying that position. When it gets down to it, every one of us are basically self-centered people. We have a bad habit of putting ourselves, our needs, our feelings, our desires, and our thoughts ahead of our spouse's. When we are both doing this, is it any wonder we can't seem to communicate or get along?

The funny thing about this concept is that when I think I am making progress, I am usually still being selfish. For example, if my wife is late coming home and I see that the kitchen is a mess, I could decide to be "selfless" and clean it "for her." First, there is some error in my approach by thinking that cleaning the kitchen is her job, so therefore if I clean it, I am doing her a big favor. Second, if I do clean it, odds are that I am going to want some recognition when she comes home. And if she fails to "thank" me, I will get mad or get my feelings hurt. Third, if I clean it, you can be guaranteed that later on that evening I will be expecting to get paid back. And if she rolls over and goes to sleep, the chances of me cleaning the kitchen the next time get very slim. You see, my selfless act was still motivated by selfishness! It is so hard to do the right thing for the right reason expecting nothing in return. Yet that is what we are called to do. The Bible says in Philippians 2:3 that we are to, "do nothing out of selfish ambition or vain conceit, but in humility consider others better than yourselves." We are not commanded to see our spouse as our equal, but as better than ourselves. Instead of selfishness we are called to sacrifice.

The **# 1 Purpose** for our marriage when it comes to the issue of esteem is submission. To submit means to "put oneself under." The definition implies a willing choice. Mark 10:45 tells us that Christ came to serve others and to give His life away. He willingly submitted Himself unto death. No one forced Him, or took His life from Him. In like manner we cannot force anyone else to submit to us, but we can model it. Ephesians 5:21 says that all of us are to submit to one another - men and women, husbands and wives. Many times we like to skip over this verse, moving on to ones that we like better, ones that serve our own purposes. We prefer verses that tell the wife to submit or ones that put the burden of Christ-like love squarely on the shoulders of the husband. We like to hold those verses up to our spouse, trying to play a little game of Biblical blackmail. We open up God's Book of love letters to us and we read each other's mail.

Instead of spending our time focusing on the responsibility of our spouse, we would be more like Jesus if we concentrated on our own need to submit. The key is mutual submission.

Learning to Encourage

Some of us need it more than others, but we are all in need of encouragement. Some even have the spiritual gift, but those who don't are not exempt or excused. It feels good to have others say positive and encouraging words to us, and the one we need to hear it from the most is our spouse. Unfortunately, many of us find it more natural and easy to criticize and tear down the one we love the most, while we strive to build up others who don't mean near as much to us.

Encouragement is not just a nice thing to do, but as believers it is our responsibility. First, it is our **Christian Responsibility**. In I Thessalonians 5:11 Paul tells us to "encourage one another and build each other up." As Christians in this world we will face adversity, temptation and ridicule. We all need our brothers and sisters in the Lord to lift us up and spur us on. That may come easy for some, but for most of us it is an art to be cultivated.

During my Bible College days I knew a man who worked hard at developing this gift. We went to the same church, and every week I would watch him as he lovingly spoke to people in the worship center, the lobby, and the parking lot. The unique thing about this particular man is that he always kept 3 x 5 index cards in his shirt pocket. As he walked away from whomever he was speaking with he would take out a card and write a note of encouragement to them concerning whatever topic they were discussing. The next day he would drop that little card in the mail. I received many a note card from him over that three year span, and every time I would be encouraged and challenged to be a better encourager myself.

Encouraging our spouse is also our **Marriage Responsibility**. If, as believers, we are given the charge to lift up the Body of Christ, how much more so should we live out that responsibility with our marriage partner? When we stood at the altar, face to face with each other, before God and man, we promised to love, honor, and cherish. Encouragement is a part of all three! My wife will not feel loved if all I do is criticize her and tear her down. She will not receive honor from me if my actions are more negative than positive. I know that she will not feel cherished if I never compliment her or build up her self-esteem.

Have you ever heard words like these: "I'm just going to go back to work, at least they like me there." or "Why do you even bother to come home when it is obvious that you would rather be with your buddies?" It is sad when we can find more encouragement from everyone else than we do each other. It is easy to let the negative comments far out weigh the positive. Sociologists tell us that we need to hear five positive things for every one negative in order for them to balance out. Given those odds, how is the health of your marital communication? We never want our spouse to look to others for the encouragement that should come from us.

Yes it is our Christian Responsibility, and it is also our Marriage Responsibility, but most importantly it is our **Love Responsibility**. Everything we have covered up to this point is why we are supposed to encourage each other. The reality is that we should want to encourage and build up the one we love the most. As a matter of fact, if we really love them it should be easy to brag on them and put them up on a pedestal. It should just pour out from the overflow of our hearts. If we can't find anything encouraging to say, then we must look at the deeper issue - the issue of the heart.

Love actively seeks ways to make the object of that love feel good. We need to look for opportunities to build up our spouse. Encouraging words need to be spoken in quiet, intimate times, shared only by the couple. We need to build up our spouse in conversation with others, never putting them down or ridiculing them. Most importantly, when we are around others and our spouse is present, we should praise them and say positive things about them, lifting them up in front of other people. In the love chapter of the Bible, I Corinthians 13, part of the definition of the word love is that it builds up.

Communicate Love

About twelve years into our marriage Pamela and I came across a book that became a mile marker for us. The book, The 5 Love Languages,[3] had a major impact on our thinking as well as our behavior. For years we had experienced times of distance and confusion, wondering why we were so far apart, and asking ourselves where the love had gone. I would sit on the couch, looking at my bride, trying to figure out why she didn't love me anymore. If I got up the courage to address the topic, her response was always the same. She would claim that I was the distant one, and that her love for me was as strong as ever. We both felt as if we were showing our love in tangible ways, but neither of us felt that love from each other. It seemed that the more we tried the more frustrated we became. Then came the book.

The premise of this book is that every person speaks primarily one of five different love languages. That is the way we communicate and receive love. The problem is that most of us marry someone who speaks a completely different language! It is as if I was speaking Spanish and Pamela was speaking French. In the long run we just didn't understand each other. Our love had not changed or drifted, but the years of miscommunication were taking their toll. Hurt and bitterness were beginning to settle into our relationship, and even though we didn't want it that way, neither of us had a clue as to how to change it. Understanding the five love languages helped us see each other in a different light, and also gave us some practical ways to deepen our love for each other.

1) Acts of Service. If this is your love language you probably enjoy doing things for your spouse. Washing the car or vacuuming the house, cleaning the bathrooms or doing the dishes, repairing things or cooking a special meal - these can all be meaningful ways of communicating love. When you do these things for your husband/wife you are saying, "See how much I love you." You feel the most loved when those kinds of things are done for you.

2) Words of Affirmation. Those who speak this love language find it natural to build others up, sharing kind, loving and positive words. Love is communicated verbally, constantly praising and complimenting those they love. They look for opportunities to encourage, and they need words of encouragement as well.

3) <u>Time</u>. Love is communicated through the quality and quantity of time spent together. It is not important what you are doing, just as long as you can be together. The time needs to be undivided and uninterrupted, with full attention devoted to each other. This includes eye contact, sharing feelings, and consistent body language. People with this love language feel closer the more time they spend together.

4) <u>Gift Giving</u>. When someone with this love language receives a gift they feel a close connection, knowing that the other person was thinking of them. It doesn't matter if the gift is big or small, expensive or cost very little. It is the act of giving that makes them feel special. They love to give gifts for no apparent reason, just to say, "I love you."

5) <u>Physical Touch</u>. This love language is self-explanatory. Love is communicated through holding hands, back rubs, light touches, hugging, kissing, and making love. Just being physically close, sitting together, arms around each other - these are the things that make them feel loved. Again, this is how they show love as well as receive it.

Think about how a couple who have completely different love languages can easily become frustrated with each other. A husband whose gift is physical touch tries to reach out to his wife whose gift is words of encouragement. He puts his arms around her and she pulls away. He tries to kiss her and she turns her head. She gives him compliments that he doesn't receive and never reciprocates. Her words fall on deaf ears and his gentle touches are rejected. A wife with the gift of service continually does kind things for her husband, who takes her for granted and expects her to do more. He takes the day off to spend with her, expressing his love through time, and she complains that he is in the way of her house cleaning.

These couples love each other, but their attempts at showing that love go unnoticed and underappreciated. The end result can be emptiness, frustration, and apathy. The answer for the pain is to learn to speak your spouse's love language. It will not be easy, but it will be worth it. Gradually we can all begin to show love to our mate in a way that makes sense to them. Understand the unique way that your husband or wife has for showing love, and receive those actions as expressions of their care for you.

Communicate Laughter

I will never forget one of the prayers the pastor prayed for Pamela and I on our wedding day. He asked God to make our home one in which laughter was heard on a daily basis. That phrase stuck in my heart, and to this day I pray that same prayer for the couples I marry. What a powerful request. I would suggest that you begin praying that prayer for your own marriage, asking God to make your home a place of fun, happiness, and joking. We have already discussed how difficult a task it is to make a marriage work. In the midst of that hard work every now and then we just need to stop and laugh.

Laughter Lightens The Load. In today's society stress is the number one killer. Laughter softens tensions and helps us lighten up a bit. It eases some of the pressures of every day life. Proverbs 17:22 says that, "a cheerful heart is good medicine, but a crushed spirit dries up the bones." Constant seriousness can become draining and overwhelming.

When we can laugh together as husband and wife we will feel closer. Sometimes we will be laughing with each other, and sometimes we may even be laughing at each other (in a nice kind of way, of course). One day Pamela was sitting at the computer and I was walking past her to get to the other side of the bed. As I made my way around her I caught my little toe on the foot of the bed. I heard it crack and dropped to my knees in pain, holding my poor little broken toe up in the air. For some warped reason my wife found this to be one of the funniest things she has ever seen! Even in my pain I couldn't help but smile because of her uncontrollable laughter.

Raising our children is a responsibility we as parents all share, and that responsibility includes discipline and correction. But what if every now and then we just sat back and laughed at their shenanigans? Would it kill us once in a while to crack up instead of getting our back up? We can probably learn some things from our kids about taking life a little less serious. John Ortberg tells a story about his little girl Mallory, and her Dee Dah Day dance. He says that whenever she feels happy and can hold it in no longer she runs around in circles singing "Dee Dah Day." One day he was just not in the mood, but Mallory was. As he was trying to dry her off after a bath she started doing the Dee Dah Day. He was irritated and quickly told her to stop and let him dry her off. Mallory looked at him and asked him "why?"

> I had no answer. I had nowhere to go, nothing to do, no meetings to attend, no sermons to write. I was just so used

to hurrying, so preoccupied with my own little agenda, so trapped in this rut of moving from one task to another, that here was life, here was joy, here was an invitation to the dance right in front of me - and I was missing it.[4]

Laughter Brightens The Building. Have you ever noticed how a cheerful face with a happy smile can light up a room? We are all drawn to happy people. No one ever sits around saying, "Man, I really want to get to know that sad looking, frowning, depressed person over there." Proverbs 15:13 says, "A happy heart makes the face cheerful, but heartache crushes the spirit." Some couples tell me they have a happy marriage, but their actions and attitudes towards each other seem to disprove their claim. Just being around them makes everybody else miserable.

We all need to smile more. We need to smile at our friends. We need to smile at our children. We need to smile at total strangers! And we really need to smile more at our spouse. Do you enjoy being married? Do you like this person you are going to stay with for the rest of your life? Do you make each other smile and laugh? If you can't answer those questions in the affirmative, then it is going to be a long, hard life.

Pamela and I lived in Memphis, Tennessee for a brief time. I will never forget the first day we arrived. It was the anniversary of Elvis Presley's death. We didn't know that at the time, but it didn't take long before that became very obvious. We checked into our motel and quickly noticed that things were a little different from what we were used to. Everywhere we looked there were Elvis Presleys. There were young Elvis' and old Elvis', there were fat Elvis' and skinny Elvis', there were white, black, and oriental Elvis', and there were even several female Elvis'. Every Elvis song ever recorded was being played in somebody's car or motel room. All of the Elvis' in the parking lot were singing, and greeting each other with a "thank ya, thank ya very much." We were extremely tired after a long day of travel, and we were anxious about our new home town, but that scene made us laugh for hours. We still laugh about it today when we think back. I'm glad I have a wife who will laugh with me, and even at me, and who makes life more fun.

Laughter Heightens The Hope. One of my favorite movies from many years ago is *The Money Pit*. The plot of the movie is that Michael Keaton and Shelley Long buy this beautiful old home that needs a little work. Before long it is obvious that they have purchased a real lemon. Everything in the house is falling apart. In one scene the electrical wiring in the kitchen shorts out and catches the whole kitchen on fire. Michael Keaton is so frustrated that he hardly even cares. He just wants to take a hot bath. As he pours the water into the tub it crashes through the floor and smashes into pieces downstairs. As he looks through the hole in the floor at the mess below he begins to chuckle. His chuckle turns into a giggle, which grows into laughter, which culminates in a hysterical belly roll, which takes his breath away. Every time I watch that movie it cracks me up. Sometimes when all seems hopeless we just have to laugh.

When a husband and wife can laugh together it can make them feel more hopeful about the future. We can't always change our circumstances, but we can change the way we view those circumstances. We can moan and groan over every bad break, or we can laugh and agree that "the sun will come out tomorrow." Oppressed or Cheerful - which one of these words best describes your marriage? Proverbs 15:15 says, "All the days of the oppressed are wretched, but the cheerful heart has a continual feast." I am so glad that God created laughter and wants us to have fun.

Communicate Life

Life is more than mere existence. We can spend years living together, and yet never experience real life. The words we communicate to each other have the power to breathe fresh life into the relationship or suck the life right out of it. Words have the power to build up or tear down, to comfort or disturb, to heal or to kill, to offer hope or bring disappointment, to express love or show hatred, to calm down or stir up, to unite or divide, to wipe away tears or cause tears to flow, to build confidence or destroy self-esteem, to restore relationships or crush them completely, to bring a smile or break a heart. Words are powerful!

With a spoken word marriages are sealed. With a spoken word marriages are ended. With a spoken word peace treaties are forged. With a spoken word wars are started. With a spoken word promises are made. With a spoken word vows are broken. With a spoken word imaginations are set free. With a spoken word dreams are dashed to pieces. I read a quote of Henry Nouwen somewhere that summed up the power of the spoken word when he said, "A little criticism makes me angry, and a little rejection makes me depressed. A little praise raises my spirits, and a little success excites me. It takes very little to raise me up or thrust me down."[5] What are we doing with our words?

One of the things that can suck the life out of marriage is **Words Harshly Spoken.** We must learn to control our tongues. The book of James says that the tongue is a fire, full of deadly poison. When we were kids we heard the saying many times, "sticks and stones may break my bones, but words will never hurt me." Nothing could be further from the truth. Painful words hurt us, they hurt our spouse, and most importantly, they hurt God. The Bible says that our words are an overflow of what is built up in our hearts, so the real issue here is deeper than just the words we communicate, it is a heart issue.

Painful, cruel, hurtful, poisonous words in marriage make healthy communication virtually impossible. We also need to realize that the pain caused by our words does not disappear with a tearful apology. There are consequences to our harsh words. Those consequences may be as minor as our own embarrassment or guilt feelings, or they could be as major as the loss of a job, the embitterment of our children, the end of a friendship, or the dissolution of our marriage. Neil Clark Warren describes the effects of anger on a relationship:

> But sometimes, in the heat of the moment when our body is burning, it feels so reasonable to let fly with a verbal left and right to the ear. Whether it's our spouse or our kids, our opponent or our colleague, our boss or our subordinate, or even God - if they haven't been meeting our needs the way we expect, or if they've been demanding too much of us and finding us inadequate, we just want to hit them squarely. Something in us presses hard to let our anger out, even though the gain will be very short-term, and the loss may hound us for a long time.[6]

A second thing that can suck the life out of marriage is **Words Hardly Spoken**. It is not enough to focus all of our attention on avoiding hurtful words. We need to concentrate on replacing those hurtful comments with positive, encouraging communication. A relationship can be just as damaged by the words we never speak as it is by the ones we do. Again, Matthew 12:34 says, "Out of the overflow of the heart the mouth speaks." If that is true of the painful comments we make that tear each other down, what does it say about the loving, uplifting words that our spouse is longing to hear? If they never hear those words coming out of our mouths, then soon they will begin to believe that those feelings do not exist in our hearts. We must convince each other of the love we have by the words we speak and the actions that accompany those words.

Is your spouse usually encouraged or discouraged by your words? Do you bring your husband/wife more smiles or more tears by the way you talk to them? Is your conversation filled with compliments or complaints? Do you focus more on the positive or the negative? Are your words "apples of gold" or "poisonous arrows?" The way you answer these questions says a lot about the kind of marriage you have.

Chapter 4

COURTSHIP

This chapter is all about the necessity of continuing a dating relationship with our spouse. It is a topic that most couples give little thought. Courting seems old fashioned, and dating is something that we leave to the young people, the single people. We're too busy raising kids and paying bills and working two jobs, we don't have time for such nonsense. After all, isn't that one of the reasons we got married in the first place - so we could get off the dating merry-go-round, and settle down into real life - married life? If that is your view of dating then please hide this book before your spouse reads this chapter. If not, you could be in for a major paradigm shift.

Consistency

Sit down with your husband/wife sometime and compare your pre and post marriage dates. That will be very difficult if you have never had any dates since you got married, but if you have had a few, how do they stack up against your single years? For most of us the picture isn't very pretty. Women, before you were married you got excited about the prospect of a date. You made sure you dressed just right, changing several times before the final presentation. You smelled really nice and looked even better. You probably tried really hard to be on time, and you were so kind and complimentary. Men, you took care of the whole evening, leaving no small detail undone. Reservations were made in advance, and behind your back were the most beautiful flowers she had ever seen. The car was gassed up (and you weren't!), and you had plenty of money to cover any unexpected charges. You were both ready and waiting, and you talked all night long.

How about those dates after you both said "I Do?" Women, if your husband does want to take you somewhere it is easy to complain that you are too tired. As far as smell goes, what's wrong with the aroma of baby spit up? And those sweat pants you are wearing are good enough for cleaning the house, and they are good enough for a date. Besides, they really are comfortable. Men, you come home from work and spring the idea on your wife that you are really in the mood for wings. Of course you don't have reservations, you don't need them for the sports bar. You definitely need to stop by the gas station on the way because the car is on fumes, and you ask your wife if she has a few bucks to spare, at least to cover the tip. You watch the game throughout the whole evening, don't say two words, and never even notice what she is wearing. She has formula on her shoulder and you have hot wing sauce on your sleeve. You truly are a match made in heaven.

Gary Chapman says that it is easy to tell which couples are married and which ones aren't when you go to a restaurant. The single couples look into each other's eyes and have long conversations. The married couples look all around the room, eat their food quickly, and hardly speak to each other. It is almost as if they went there to eat![1] You see, it is not just about the act of dating, it is really about the attitude of dating. It's an issue of importance.

The first thing that must be present if our dating lives are going to improve is that it must be a **Priority**. It is true that we all make time for what we really want to do. I may tell everyone that I don't have enough time to mow the lawn, but I will make sure I block out three hours to watch the ball game. If you and your spouse are going to have a dating life that is vibrant and fun it is going to have to be important to you both. You have to make it a regular part of your life. You can even put your dates on your calendar. When my wife and I first talked about scheduling some of our dates I hated the idea. It seemed too much like a business appointment. When I complained, Pamela told me that she would rather me put her name down in my DayTimer than come to the end of the month and realize that we never got around to spending any time together. If we don't do this we end up settling for trying to squeeze in a date or two in our-left over time. We must look at this like we do our tithe. God wants our first fruits, our best, not our leftovers. In the same way our spouse deserves our best, our quality time, not just a few hours we can steal every now and then.

It is so easy to take each other for granted. We didn't do that when we were dating. By the way, why do we use that phrase - "when we were dating?" It implies that we don't do that any more. It is a thing of the past, a part of our single years, a part that is no longer important. Why was dating so important before we got married? Most of us would agree that the time we spent together allowed us to get to know each other better, to develop a relationship. If that is true, then what are we saying to each other if we no longer date? "Honey, I think I know you about as well as I want to." "Babe, I am not sure that continuing to develop our relationship is much of a priority for me any more." Wow! I don't think that is a message any of us want to send. Dating was vitally important before we got married, and it is even more so now that we are. Granted, it was easier to date before we had kids, but it is even more important after our children come along. If you have kids and you never date, I guarantee that very soon you will go completely insane! You have got to get out of the house.

Our dating life needs to be a priority, and some of our dates need to be **Planned**. Not all of our dates have to be special, but they should all be "special." Why? Because the one we are with is special. Not every date has to be big and expensive. Some can be picnics or bike rides or a movie rental and a pizza. But sometimes we need to pull out the big guns. Sometimes we need to spend more money than we think we should just to communicate to our spouse that we think she is worth it. Sometimes we need to plan out our dates, think them out, set aside plenty of time. It is fun to ask your husband/wife on a date. The advanced planning can lead to anticipation and excitement. It gives you both something to look forward to. Spontaneous dates are fun, and we will talk about that later, but it is easy to get into a rut of last minute, boring, routine dates, with each person trying to come up with something to do.

Dating should be a priority and we should take time to plan some special dates, but we also need to make sure that we are **Prepared**. When our children are small, one of the most difficult aspects of dating is childcare. We can communicate a lot to our spouse if we will line up a baby sitter in advance. This is not just the woman's job. Guys, we will score some major points with our wife if we take care of this detail ourselves. I can't tell you how many times I told Pamela I would take care of this, but then waited until the day before to start making calls. It is amazing how many teenage girls make plans more than a day in advance. I guess I thought they would just be sitting around awaiting my invitation to spend quality time with the two most beautiful kids in the world! That doesn't appear to be the case.

Being prepared for a date means going to the bank beforehand, not pooling your cash together in the car on the way. It means making reservations, buying tickets in advance, knowing the show times, and being ready in plenty of time. A big part of a successful date is preparing the mood. This is an all day adventure. We cannot argue with each other all day and expect to have a romantic evening. We need to work at establishing that emotional connection, preparing ourselves emotionally for the time we will spend together. Again let me say that all dates don't need to be expensive. Some of the most special times I can remember with my wife are long walks on the beach, picnics and bike rides, and ice cream cones on a summer night. However, periodically it doesn't hurt to drop a few bucks, dress up, and go out on the town. Either way, we need to make sure that we are consistently dating.

Creativity

Consistency is great, but if we're not careful it is easy to become consistently boring. We made a promise to each other that we were going to go on a date twice a month, and by golly we are going to keep that promise whether we want to or not! We pick up the baby sitter at 6:00, we make the 7:00 movie, and we stop for a late night bite before we head home. That was fun now, wasn't it? Creativity takes time and effort, but boredom takes very little of either. Dating is good, but dating for the sole purpose of saying that we did so doesn't really help us much. We must be creative. We can plan creatively and we can be creatively impulsive.

Pamela and I are very different people who like very different things. I love watching sports and she loves watching old movies. I am most alive in the morning, while she gets her energy late at night. I love the fall and winter, she loves spring and summer. Rock and Roll is my preference, but she enjoys Country music. I want to be the life of the party and she is content to stay behind the scenes. We even have totally different ideas as to what a fun vacation should look like. Pamela loves a vacation that is planned down to the last detail. She wants to know where we are going, where we are staying, when and what we are eating, and what activities we will be enjoying. She knows what time we will wake up and what time we will go to sleep. That is her perfect vacation. That sounds exhausting to me. By the time I read all of those details I feel like I've already gone and come back! There's no use in even going. Now, my idea of a fun vacation is completely the opposite. I like to come home from work and just announce that everyone needs to pack, because we are taking off for a few days. I am not sure exactly where we are going or how long we will stay. We'll figure that out when we get there. I want to wake up when I wake up, go to bed when I get sleepy, eat when I get hungry, and roll over when I start burning. When we run out of money it is time to go home. Wow! That sounds fantastic.

Maybe that is a little extreme for some of you, but the main point is that sometimes we need to be **Spontaneous.** Some of our dates do need to be carefully planned and prepared for, but not all of them. Some need to be spur of the moment, no idea what we are going to do next, fly by the seat of your pants, wild and crazy dates. Spontaneity creates a freedom in marriage, a free spirit waiting to be released. Sometimes we need to have spontaneous dates, and sometime we need a little spontaneity on our dates. Have you ever been driving around look over and see a fountain, and just decide it would be fun to kick off your shoes, roll up your pants legs, and splash around together? Or maybe it's already 11:00 PM and you both just decide to drive downtown, get an ice cream, and sit on a park bench for hours? Granted, these kinds of dates are easier before you have kids, or after they are grown, but you get the picture.

Spontaneity means that you communicate to your spouse that you are open to suggestions. It means that you want your relationship to always be fresh and exciting. It means that you are going to fight against the tendency to fall into ruts and allow the life to stop flowing through your marriage. Some of my favorite married dates with Pamela were sitting on the steps of the Capitol building in Columbia, S.C. for hours, eating ice cream cones and talking about our future. We loved going to the airport, watching all the planes and all the people. Sometimes we would make plans but then change them mid date, and do something completely different. It wasn't really about what we were doing, it was about who we were doing it with.

Romance is another important ingredient in dating. Flowers, cards, candy, and love poems don't have to stop once we put a ring on each other's finger. Loving little surprises, small gifts, phone calls, long walks and holding hands, are all vital parts of a growing marriage. We need to take time to look into each other's eyes, say all the things we haven't said in a long time, and share fond memories of times gone by. Don't save romance for Valentines Day or anniversaries. It's nice then, but it will mean even more if we are romantic for no reason at all. Most of us don't ever want the sexual aspect of our marriage to fade away, but we put very little effort into setting the mood, creating the right atmosphere, that fans the sexual flame. I think this is an area where all of us could use some help, especially all of us guys.

Let me make a brilliant observation here - dating should be **Fun**! Our marriage should be the most fun relationship we have. If our dates aren't fun then nobody is going to want to go. We need to laugh and joke and do things that we both love to do. Sit down with your spouse and make a list of at least ten things you would both enjoy doing together. There - you've got your dates lined up for the next year. One more thing - now that we are married we can have over night dates! That wasn't allowed before, but now it is encouraged. We get to have a fun time together, drive our date home, and then go to bed with her! It doesn't get any better than that.

Courtesy

The definition of the word courteous means, "gracious, good manners, consideration and respect for others." Do we treat each other with courtesy? We probably did before we got married, or we would still be single. Are we always considering their desires ahead of our own? Ladies, do you go with your husband to the ball game, even though there are many more places you would rather be? Men, do we dress up and attend the musical with our wife, even though we would never choose that for a date? Do we have articles of clothing that our spouse hates, but we continue to wear them out in public because they are comfortable?

Let's take the issue of **Hygiene**. When we were single and preparing for a date most of us would spend hours "prettying up." We would shower and shave and spray on smelly stuff. Our hair looked perfect, we made sure our clothes were clean and ironed, we brushed our teeth and used mouthwash, and double checked our deodorant, just in case. What about now that we are married? If we think the absence of those things would be offensive to a date, what makes us think that it won't bother our spouse? If we don't care about how we look or smell when we go on a date with our spouse, it sends a clear message to them that they are not very important. Trust me, it is not the message we want to be sending.

Likewise, what about **Manners**? I know it sounds kind of silly to be talking to grown ups about manners, but unfortunately we don't all act like grownups. For some reason women just don't seem to care too much for belching, scratching, and bodily noises. They don't even like it at a ball game, much less a date. Chewing with our mouths open or picking our nose doesn't go very far toward setting the romantic mood. Some of us are worse at this than others. My biggest flaw when it comes to manners is the bad habit of picking my teeth after we eat. It drives Pamela crazy! It's one thing if I wait until we leave the restaurant and grab a toothpick as we are going out the door. It is another when I sit at the table using a straw, a business card, a fork, or whatever else I can find to relieve myself of unwanted leftovers. She just doesn't find that attractive.

There is also the lost art of **Chivalry**. You know - bravery, honor, devotion - being a gentleman. Chivalry may be dead, but we as Christian men to revive it. In 1996 the Olympics came to Atlanta. Pamela and I decided that we wanted to go downtown and wander around in the crowd, watching the people from all over the world. We got on MARTA, our rapid transit system, and tried to find a spot to sit down. It was packed, but we found two seats. Just before the doors shut a woman stepped aboard the train. I stood up and offered her my seat. I am not sure what country she was from, but in her strong accent she declined my offer. I insisted, and she reluctantly sat down. She looked to my wife and said that never in her life had a man stood up and offered a seat to her before. She said, "I didn't think that happened any more." That's sad. As my children were younger we regularly attended awards day programs at school. Each and every time there would be women standing while men sat down. Not just women, but pregnant women and elderly women, all standing up through an entire program while able bodied men sat there without even flinching. Right here in the

South - can you believe it?! My daddy would have whipped me severely if I had ever done anything like that.

Well what about dates with our wives? Are we chivalrous? Do we always stand up so our lady can sit? Do we take off our coat and wrap it around her shoulders if she is cold, or do we mock her and say, "I told you it was going to be cold. You should have brought your own."? Do we open the car door so she can get in or out? Ladies, do you let your husband do those things for you? I once heard a quote that said, "If a man opens the car door for his wife you can be sure one of two things is true. He either has a new car or a new wife." That is just not right.

Have you ever noticed that there are different dating personalities? Some people are the *pleasers*. Whenever you are trying to decide which restaurant to pick they always say, "whatever you want." They never want to voice their own opinion. It's not that they don't have one, they just don't share it. You know how it goes - "Hey honey, what do you want to eat?" "Oh, it doesn't matter, whatever you want." "Well, I was thinking Chinese." "Oh, not Chinese. I don't think I could handle that tonight." "Okay. What would you like?" "It doesn't matter. Whatever you want." "Well, how about seafood?" "No, I just had seafood yesterday." "Okay. What would you like?" "It doesn't matter. You choose." "For Pete's sake, just tell me what you want!" That is just not fun. Then there are the *controllers*. They always want to choose. Whenever you are trying to pick a place to go they always say, "whatever I want." Maybe the last four or five movies the two of you have seen together were all the kind of movies she likes, but when you tell her you want to see a comedy instead of a chick flick she bristles at the idea. She tells you that you are too immature and that she will not sit through one of your mindless, slapstick films, just because you seem to find them humorous. So once again you back down and watch the movie of her choice. That gets old after a while. Then there are the *withholders*. When the two of you are deciding how to spend your evening they just say, "whatever." They are completely disconnected, clearly communicating their apathy towards the whole situation. It's not that they are trying to be nice and giving, they just don't care. It is as if spending time with you is an inconvenience, something they wish they could get out of. Now there is someone that is going to be a fun date! It would be more fun staying home and washing clothes. At least then you would be accomplishing something.

We should all be striving to become *genuine lovers*. People who long to spend time with each other, eagerly anticipating the evening. It doesn't really matter where we go as long as we are together, but we do want to clearly voice our excitement for the upcoming evening. We share from our hearts some things we would enjoy doing, while being open to doing the exact opposite if that is what our spouse wants. The point is that your date is the object of your attention, not whatever activity you choose. When two genuine lovers have a date it will always be a success, whether it was a walk in the park or dancing the night away, because they focused on each other.

To wrap up this whole idea of dating let's look at that famous passage of Scripture dealing with marriage in Revelation 2:4,5. Okay, so it's not about marriage, but I do believe that the principles Christ shares about our relationship with Him can be applied to our relationship with our spouse. Jesus, speaking to the church at Ephesus, basically says that although they had done a lot of good things, there was still one area in which they were falling short. He told them that they had forgotten their first love. He also gave them a three-fold plan as to how they could restore that initial relationship with Him. He said, "remember the height from which you've fallen, repent, and do the things you did at first." That sounds like a good plan for marriage.

When we have lost our first love with our spouse we need to follow Jesus' directions very closely. The first thing He says we must do is *remember*. Many times I talk to couples who have a lot going for them, but their biggest problem is that they have forgotten their first love. As a matter of fact, sometimes they use this as their excuse for divorce. The husband will look at me and say, "John, the problem is that I just don't love her anymore." I always try to respond to that statement with as much tact and sympathy as I can. I will usually say, "So. What has that got to do with anything? You stood up before a lot of people and God and promised you would love her until you die, so start doing it." When he realizes that is not going to work with me he pulls out the big gun. He says, "Well John, to tell you the truth, I don't think I ever really loved her." I will look him straight in the face and reply, "Well then, I guess you are probably the biggest fool I may have ever met. You dated this girl for two years, were engaged to her for ten months, planned a wedding, got married, had three kids, and lived with her for fifteen years, and you never even loved her! Wow!" No, the problem isn't that he never loved her. The problem is that it has been so long since he has felt any love that he can't even remember what it was like.

This couple needs to take some time and reminisce about their early years together. They should pull out the old photo albums and share stories about times that were meaningful to them. They must remember better times, and determine to find them again. The second thing Christ said we should do is *repent*. We need to repent to God and each other for all the things we have done as well as all the things we have neglected doing that have pushed us apart. Everyone has regrets, and sometimes we just need to stop and tell each other that we are sorry. Over the years bitterness begins to grow and becomes a cancer to the relationship. We must genuinely be broken for all the pain we have caused, and seek to restore the closeness we once had.

The third step in Christ's plan is that we *renew*. He tells us to "do the things we did at first." We need to renew our love the same way we initially grew it. When we were first dating and newly married we took walks together and sang songs to each other and held hands and wrote notes and talked on the phone for hours. Most of us can't remember the last time we did any thing like that. If those are the kind of things that drew us to each other in the first place, then what makes us believe that the same kinds of things can't make us feel close once again? We need to make a new commitment to dating and spending time together, talking and looking into each other's eyes, and rebuilding that love that once stood tall and strong. It won't be easy at first. We used to date because we wanted to, now we should date because we need to, but if we keep it up long enough, that desire should return and we will once again enjoy our dating life.

Chapter 5

CONFLICT

We have already stated the statistics concerning the struggles of marriages in America. Around 50% of first marriages fail, and that number increases with each succeeding marriage.[1] On a daily basis police reports are filed for spousal abuse, threats of physical harm, and domestic disputes. Temporary protective orders are written and served, and couples are mandated to Anger Management courses and Family Violence groups. Sometimes the conflict even results in death. Many violent crimes happen among family members. Marital conflict does not always take such a destructive form, but arguing and fighting without knowing how to resolve the issues can slowly erode the love and connection.

Reasons for Conflict

How we handle conflict is essential when it comes to the health of our marriages. Most couples who come in for counseling say that their number one problem area is a lack of communication, followed closely by the inability to resolve conflict. The goal of this chapter is to help couples understand the reasons behind all the arguing, to help them see how they react to it, and to help them learn how to resolve their differences. Learning to work through our difficulties is a good indicator of the future success or demise of our relationship. Conflict, in and of itself, is not a bad thing, but if it is not controlled it can be destructive. When handled correctly conflict can ultimately produce closeness and unity. In order to find victory in this area of our marriage we must first take a look at several problems that can lead to conflict.

Past Problems: We cannot separate who we are from how we were raised. The differences in our background, culture, and family of origin, can lead to disagreements and arguments. Most couples learned very different communication styles growing up. If one spouse was raised in a single parent home or blended family, and the other grew up with both of their biological parents, they could see marriage or family through a different set of lens. Both of Pamela's parents worked outside of the home as she was growing up, whereas my family consisted of a dad who left for work each morning and a stay at home mom. Those differences have created in us individual expectations that affect our own marriage. Some people enter marriage with past baggage from previous failed relationships. Those issues do not disappear with a new marriage license. Some people's family of origin was structured and legalistic while others grew up in a more liberal, relaxed atmosphere. If a husband was raised by parents who showered him with love and affection, and his wife grew up in a cold, distant family, that was not outwardly loving or touchy, their relationship is in for some bumps in the road. These past problems may be valid reasons for our conflict, but we must never allow them to become excuses. We cannot change the past, but we can choose to leave the past in the past.

Perfection Problems: Many of us come into the marital relationship with a wrong view of marriage, one that is filled with unrealistic expectations. We begin this new union by placing such high demands on each other that there is almost no chance for success. It is easy for us to base these expectations on worldly values and models. I have already mentioned the problem of comparing our marriage to what we read about in romance novels and skin magazines. The people portrayed in these types of publications are not real. They are faultless, air brushed, imaginary ideas from the depravity of other people's minds. It is wrong for us to compare our spouse to the ones we see on television or at the movies. This is real life, warts and all. Expectations of perfection will always lead to marital frustration. Besides, we all know that if our spouse perfected all the things we love to complain about, it wouldn't take long before we found some other area with which we are not happy. The key here is learning to be satisfied with the one God has given to us.

Perspective Problems: It is clear that the same event can be seen from several different angles. One wreck could have four eye witnesses who all have their own opinion as to what really happened. In marriage, no one person is always right, no matter what some of us like to think. Many times our arguments are not even an issue of right and wrong, they are just a matter of opinion and perspective. For example, Pamela and I seemed to never agree about our daughter's sense of humor when she was younger. I can remember many nights around the dinner table discussing the way that Abigail was talking to us, and the things she was saying. Pamela felt like she was a smart mouth and was waiting on me to correct her. I thought she was hilarious and was trying to not burst out in laughter. Needless to say, that was a source of conflict in our relationship. When it comes to a difference of opinion we need to ask ourselves one simple question. Do we want to be right or do we want to be happy? The answer to that question will determine the direction of the conflict.

Personality Problems: I have already discussed the issue of personality differences, going into a little detail about the DISC profiles. I believe this is a major source of marital conflict. Most marriages are made up of distinctly different personality types. We were drawn to each other because of those differences, but after living together for a while those same cute qualities begin to grate on our nerves. The differences in my own marriage were clear from the very beginning. I was extremely outgoing and Pamela was extremely introverted. I had a habit on Sundays of walking up and down the church isles greeting people and striking up conversations. Pamela had a habit of shadowing my every move, walking directly behind me every step of the way. It drove me crazy. One day I turned around and told her to get a life, get some friends, and give me some space! (That was my sensitive nature coming out. After all, my number one spiritual gift really is mercy.) We have struggled over the years accepting each other the way we are, and even learning to celebrate our differences. Sometimes we do better than others, and sometimes we allow those differences to turn into hurtful arguments.

Priority Problems: Our values and convictions can be a source of conflict as well. Some things that are absolutes to one person may just be optional to the other. Can you imagine the tension at home when a wife views family dinner time as a non-negotiable, while the husband believes that it's fine for each family member to eat whenever and wherever they would like? What about when a husband believes strongly in the value of saving money, but his wife is a spend-thrift? Sometimes even our spiritual convictions can be a sore spot in the marriage. Take for instance a wife who feels strongly that she and her husband should tithe, while her husband does not hold to that same belief. If one spouse places a high priority on encouraging the children to spend time each day reading, and the other spouse sees nothing wrong with allowing the kids to watch television from the moment they come home from school until they go to bed, there will be conflict in the home. Family traditions that are crucial to one spouse may seem trivial to the other. Even fun times like the holidays can turn into major arguments if the couple does not agree with how they should spend those days. Priorities that are not agreed upon going into the marriage can later put pressure on the relationship.

Perception Problems: Some people are contemplative, thinking through every situation, weighing all the options, before ever making a decision. Others are more impulsive, going with their gut feelings, trusting everything to work out in the long run. Which one is right? Not necessarily either of them, but if they marry each other, they are in for many long battles. Assumptions can play a destructive role in relationships as well. A wife is quiet and reflective, enjoying a peaceful moment, but her husband is convinced she is mad at him. He follows her around the house asking what is wrong, refusing to accept her answer. He persists so much that finally he gets his wish - now she is mad. What one sees as a quiet mood the other sees as a moody spouse. There is not a real problem, just a perceived one. But before long that perception leads to real trouble. Assumptions are dangerous.

Petty Problems: These problems are sometimes the worst. Little, nit-picky, unimportant issues that get blown out of proportion and twisted around until they cause serious damage. Intelligent people can get all bent out of shape about whether the toilet paper roll is supposed to come over the top or go underneath instead. Couples can go for days without speaking to each other because one of them misplaced the T.V. remote. Make-up on the counter, clothes on the floor, and the failure to push the dresser drawer all the way in, can seem as important as the budget or the children's education. Pamela and I used to argue about the way we each dispensed the toothpaste. She always squeezes from the middle, while I think you should roll it neatly from the end. We decided the best way to solve that problem was for us each to have our own tube of toothpaste! It works. We need to stop arguing about things that aren't worth arguing over. We shouldn't allow the minors to become majors. There are enough major issues to occupy our time.

Reacting To Conflict

Couples come in to see me on a regular basis, and many times the issue they want to discuss is conflict. Periodically I meet a couple who tell me that they never fight. In those cases I have found one of three things to be true. Some couples never argue because there is no passion in their marriage. Most couples who love passionately argue passionately. A couple who never experiences conflict doesn't have very much emotional investment in the marriage. Some couples never argue because there is no equality in their relationship. One person tells the other what to do and they do it. When one person dominates another, never allowing them to voice an opinion or raise any objections, there will be no outward conflict. Finally, if a couple tells me they never argue there is always the possibility that there is no truth in their statement. Some people live in denial and try to convince others to buy into their deception as well. For this couple, conflict is not their biggest problem, lying is.

If we are sick and go to the doctor for medication, we hope that we will respond well to that prescription. Periodically we have a reaction to the medicine, which leads to even bigger problems. That is a major problem when it comes to conflict - many times we react to it instead of responding to it. Relationship equals conflict. It is impossible to have a relationship in which there is truth, equality, and emotional investment, and not face some degree of conflict. The only question is, how will we handle it? The way we deal with our disagreements is determined in large degree by our family of origin. We learn how to argue by watching our parents. Some of us become just like them, and some of us become just the opposite. Some people tell me the reason they yell and scream is because their parents yelled and screamed. Others will say that because their parents acted that way they will never raise their voice. There are several ways to react to conflict. I believe there are two extremes.

The first extreme way of reacting to conflict is seen in those people who **Avoid** a fight. They hate conflict, and will do anything to keep from being in an argument. If that means always giving in, then they will give in. If that means emotionally shutting down, never sharing their feelings, then that is what they will do. By doing so, this type of person believes they are being mature or spiritual. They see themselves as the one in the relationship who is dealing with the problems correctly. After all, they are not the ones wanting to fight. In reality, the avoider is not motivated by strength but by fear. They feel anger, but are afraid to face it. They stuff their feelings deep down, out of sight and mind, but the result is bitterness and resentment. This destructive pattern leads to built up anger that will come out somehow. If they continue doing this, ultimately they will shut down all of their feelings and emotionally check out of the relationship.

It is important for us to realize that the opposite of love is not hate, it is apathy. When couples come to my office with red faces, hurt feelings, and hearts racing, I know that there is still hope. There are some feelings present, albeit negative ones. But, when a couple comes in and one or both people have emotionally given up, the chances for salvaging the relationship are less encouraging. Les and Leslie Parrot say that conflict can lead couples into a deeper sense of intimacy.[2] At a conference I attended I heard Les say that "the path to intimacy is conflict." What they are saying is that the way we develop an intimate relationship is through processing conflict in a constructive way, not avoiding it. If we think about those we are closest to we are forced to acknowledge this truth. We all have many acquaintances, people with whom we have a surface relationship. We never argue with them, but we don't have any level of intimacy with them either. The deeper the relationship, the more intimate we are with a person, the more conflict is usually present. Now remember, the Parrotts are not saying that the more conflict you have the closer you will be. If that were true I know a lot of really close couples! The point they are making is that the better we learn to work through our conflict the closer we will be. Couples who have faced serious problems, and with the Lord's help have survived, form a bond that strengthens their marriage. The next time troubles come they know that they can make it.

The second extreme way of reacting to conflict is seen in those people who **Adore** a fight. They seem to love conflict and are always looking for trouble. Their personality is argumentative, and they enjoy playing the role of instigator. It is easier for this type person to see the negative in their relationship rather than the positive. The key problem is one of attitude that leads to actions. Each one of us need to realize the danger of negative self-talk and consciously defend ourselves against it. We can all allow ourselves to fall into the trap of negativity and criticism, focusing on the things we dislike about our spouse and overlooking all of their positive character qualities. Soon, if not checked, this can become habit forming. We need to develop a plan, a spiritual plan for winning this spiritual battle.

Let me illustrate by giving several scenarios. Scenario number one: I leave work after a fifteen hour day, exhausted, and ready to be home. As I get into the car I say to myself, "When I get home, the house had better be clean. I've worked all day long and Pamela has been home. I don't want to find dishes in the sink or any clothes on the floor." With that thought running through my mind I drive home. When I open the back door, there they are - dirty dishes piled high in the sink! The odds are slim that we will have a good evening, regardless of the reasons for the mess. Scenario number two: I leave work, get in the car, and have the same negative conversation with myself. When I get home I find the house spotless. Will I have a good evening with my wife? Maybe, but my attitude is still one that says, "You had better be glad you cleaned up." Scenario number three: I leave work, get into the car, and begin praying, "Lord, I am so exhausted. I know that it would be very easy for me to get home and act like a jerk. Please help me treat Pamela with love and respect no matter what the house looks like. She is a great wife who always keeps the house clean. If it is dirty tonight that means she has really had a rough day. Help me be supportive." I get home, open the back door, and find the house a mess. I walk in, put my arms around my wife and say, "I bet you've had a hard day. Why don't you sit down and relax and let me clean up the kitchen." She will reply, "No, you sit down and let me get it. I'm sorry about the house. I know that bothers you, but I have not been home all day. One of the kids came home sick from school, we went to the doctor and pharmacy, your mother called, I worked on the bills, and the day just got away from me." Then together we could clean the kitchen while we discussed the details of our day. Scenario number four: Same as number three except for the spotless house I find when I get home. I walk in the door, thank Pamela for how wonderful the house looks, and we sit together discussing our day.

The point of those scenarios is that the success of our evening has very little to do with the appearance of our house, and has everything to do with my attitude. If I go home looking for a fight the odds are pretty high that I will find one. The better we learn to work through our disagreements the less fights we will have. The amount and intensity of conflict should decrease over the years. I don't believe there will ever come a day when our marriage will be conflict free, but I do believe that we can argue less and less and resolve those arguments quicker. That is one of the goals of our marriage.

Resolution Of Conflict

When it comes to marital conflict the key is not to avoid it or adore it, but to resolve it. We need to learn how to work through our issues together, allowing each other to share thoughts, feelings, and differing opinions without getting defensive or critical. This is a skill few of us were ever taught. We know how to fight, but we don't know how to fight fair. It is obvious that our current approach to conflict isn't working, but we keep "dancing" that destructive dance. It is time we learned some new steps. The following is a seven step method for handling conflict that I like to call "Fight Night."

1) Accepting The Challenge: The Heavy Weight Champion of the World doesn't accept every challenge to defend his title. He only accepts the ones that will be beneficial. Our marriages could learn a lot from his example. Just because an argument raises its ugly head does not mean that we must have a fight. We need to learn to pick our battles. We know this principle when it comes to our children, but it is vitally important that we apply it to our marriages as well. Whenever we begin to get angry we need to stop and ask ourselves if this issue is worth arguing over. The reality is that many are not. If we fight over every little issue then the important ones get lost in the shuffle. Some things are so insignificant that it is foolish to allow them to become a source of conflict. We can all remember times after a major argument, replaying it through our minds, wondering how we allowed something so trivial to become so hurtful. Proverbs 20:3 says, "It is to a man's honor to avoid strife, but every fool is quick to quarrel."

2) Time For The Main Event: When we ask ourselves if an issue is worth arguing over, sometimes the answer will be a resounding "yes." If we believe this issue is one that must be dealt with, we need to ask ourselves a second question. That question is, "Is now the best time for an argument?" Timing is everything. Is this a good time for you both, a time when you can address this issue with no distractions? I know that's a hard question to ask, given the fact that we don't plan our arguments, they just happen. However, some times are just not conducive to arguing. Late at night when one person is almost asleep. Early in the morning when one of you is definitely not a morning person. When one of you is sick, or preoccupied, or stressed. Maybe you are running late, on your way to church, in a public place, or around other people. Someone needs to speak up and ask for a better time. The person who asks to postpone the argument must also suggest a better time, some time within 24 hours, when they promise to sit down and deal with the issue. Coming back to the problem at a better time will allow you both to focus on the issue rather than the timing. Also, by postponing some arguments there is always the chance that the needed space could completely diffuse the argument all together. Ecclesiastes 3:1 says, "There is a time for everything, and a season for every activity under heaven."

3) Prize Money: Professional boxers don't fight just for the thrill of hitting someone else. They know that if they are good enough there is a reward in store. Here is the question regarding marital conflict, "What are we fighting for?" What is it that we hope to get out of this argument. If we are honest, most of us would say that we are in it to win it. We think we are right and we want to prove our point. If our goal is to win the argument then we have already lost. Tim Kimmel spoke at our church several years ago. I will never forget what he said concerning this topic. He said, "if we win every argument with our spouse then we are sleeping with a loser!" Good point. Our only true battle aim should be to better understand each other and their point of view. We know the rule of communication that says, "seek first to understand, then to be understood," but it is a difficult rule to apply. Some of us will claim a loftier goal. We will say that we don't want to win, we just want to be heard. That sounds better, but the reality is that if our goal is to be heard, we will interrupt, raise our voice, and demand that our spouse be quiet and let us speak. It is still a selfish motive. A better motive is to listen to and hear our spouse's view point, whether we agree with it or not. Romans 14:19 says, "Let us make every effort to do what leads to peace and mutual edification."

4) No Hitting Below The Belt: It's okay to be angry as long as we don't allow that anger to turn destructive. We need to make sure that this argument is a clean fight. That means that we must check

our weapons often. It is easy for most of us to pull out all the stops
and come kicking and screaming when we feel like our back is up
against the rope. Each one of us possess unique yet painful arguing
tools. We yell and scream, call names, throw things, slam doors, use
put downs or sarcasm, pout, accuse, point fingers, roll eyes, give the
silent treatment, bring up the past, or just walk away. This list is certainly not all inclusive, but it is a sample of some of the hurtful things
we do to each other in the midst of an argument. We need to ask
our husband or wife what it is that we do when we are fighting that
is hurtful to them. Then we need to give each other permission to
point that out to us in a loving way the next time we use that weap-
on in an argument. Habits will take a while to break, and we must
be patient with each other, allowing room for failure. But with time
we want to break those destructive patterns and replace them with
healthier ones. Ephesians 4:26 says, "In your anger do not sin."

5) At The Sound Of The Bell: If you have ever watched a boxing
match you have seen one guy pounding on another up against
the ropes when the bell rings. What happens? He stops hitting him,
right? Wrong. He is supposed to stop, but usually he gets in another
punch or two before the referee pulls him away. That resembles
too closely many of our marital arguments. When one of us has the
other up against the ropes we don't want to back away or give
them some space. We want to go in for the kill. Instead we need to
learn how to ask for and give each other a time out. A time out is a
brief breather, a break from the argument to clear our heads and
adjust our attitudes. It is not quitting, nor is it a time to simmer and
reload. We ask for a time out whenever we feel like we are about to

say something we will regret, or when we feel backed into a corner and need some space. We need to walk out on the porch, count to ten, say a quick prayer, and take some deep breaths. It's hard to ask for a time out, but it's even harder to give one. When our spouse asks for some space we must give it to them. Whoever asks for the time out must come back in ten minutes or so and resume the discussion, hopefully with clearer heads and a resolved spirit to work through the issue. Even if we can't completely resolve the issue we need to calmly agree to set it aside, and not walk away angry and bitter. Ephesians 4:26 says, "Do not let the sun go down while you are still angry."

6) Who's In Your Corner? It is essential that we never reveal the details of our private matters to others. Airing our dirty laundry to family, friends, or coworkers will only end up alienating our spouse and harming our relationship. It is one thing to have a trusted friend with whom you can turn when things at home are not going well, someone you can ask to pray for you when you are sad or hurting, but it is another to tell that trusted friend all the details of your disagreements, breaking trust with your spouse and putting a wedge between them and the one with whom you shared. Besides, most of us like to share with people who will see things from our perspective, and ultimately their support for our position pours gasoline on our already out of control fire. I believe that if couples talked to each other about their struggles as much as they talked to others that those struggles would be resolved quicker and hurt less. The best way to earn the respect of our spouse is to make a commitment to never break their confidence. Proverbs 20:19 says, "A gossip betrays a confidence."

7) No Rematch: Once the issue has been resolved it should never be brought up again unless both husband and wife agree. It is not fair to dig it back up later and throw it in each other's face. It is not healthy. I have found that when you dig up dead things they stink. Things that are buried need to remain buried. We need to leave the past in the past. True forgiveness leaves no room for holding grudges or dwelling in the past. Bringing up the past puts our spouse at an unfair disadvantage. We have a tendency to use our past arguments to supplement our present ones, instead of allowing each disagreement to stand on its own. Living in the past prevents happiness in the present and offers no hope of a future. Colossians 3:13 says, "Bear with each other and forgive whatever grievances you may have against one another."

Chapter 6

CONFESSION

Wouldn't it be wonderful if we could go through our marriage without ever messing up? Can you imagine how good our relationship would be if we could do everything right, always treat each other with respect, never lose our temper or say things we shouldn't say? What if no husband ever made his wife cry or no wife ever made her husband so mad that he just wanted to go back to work? Think about a home where there are never any harsh words, selfish acts, or hurt feelings. Can you picture it? I can't! That's not real life.

Acceptance of Fallibility

Real marriage is made up of two imperfect people with selfish agendas and fallen sin natures. We are not perfect and, this side of Heaven, never will be. We are human beings, warts and all. The sooner we learn to accept that fact the better chance our marriage has for success. Sometimes it is hard to accept that fact about our spouse, putting them so high up on a pedestal that when they fall we are crushed. Sometimes it is hard to accept that fact about ourselves, sugar coating our mistakes and minimizing our weaknesses. Living in this fantasy world sets us up for failure. What do we need to do? How do we make our marriage that is filled with flaws last a lifetime?

The first thing we have to do is deal with the **Reality Of Sin**. Romans 3:23 says that all of us have sinned and fall short of God's glory. Part of a healthy marriage is understanding that the person we are married to is a sinner, just like us. We all fail God and we all fail each other. This is not an excuse, and it is certainly not a license for apathy or irresponsibility, but it is a fact of life. Allowing each other to be human, accepting the fact that sometimes we will make poor choices, exhibit wrong behavior, and express bad attitudes, keeps us humble and totally dependant on God. It is easier for us to make allowances for our children and our friends than it is each other.

Two sinful people filled with pride, anger, and selfishness, choosing to live together in marriage, is an arrangement that results in failures, disappointment, and pain. If we are believers we have no choice but to acknowledge that we fail God, but sometimes it is harder for us to see and admit to the pain we cause each other. Admitting our sinful nature forces us to our knees, asking God to continue His work in us, molding us into the kind of husband or wife He desires of us. It requires us to do periodic self check-ups, honestly evaluating the progress we are making when it comes to being a spirit-controlled spouse. Just like A.A., admitting that we have a problem is the first step toward recovery.

Another important step in the process of accepting each other's faults is recognizing our own **Unrealistic Expectations**. Not only do we fall short of God's glory, we also fall short of each other's expectations, hopes, and dreams. Most of us entered marriage with rose-colored glasses, assuming that our marriage would be better than anything we had ever imagined. Years of witnessing other marital failures strengthened our resolve to make our own marriage perfect.

Television and movies gave us examples of what a marriage should be, and we planned on following that script down to the very last page. Sure, other husbands complained about the sexual coldness of their wife, but we were positive that problem would never enter our bedroom. Of course we had listened to other wives complain about the lack of romance in their relationship, but we just knew that our romantic ways would get stronger after we said "I do." It was obvious that communication could prove to be difficult, but we were both committed to working on it regularly. Our marriage was going to be different. It didn't take long before we began feeling bitterness and resentment over the broken promises and lack of effort that we saw in each other. We felt lied to and deceived, living with disappointment and hurt over unmet needs and unfulfilled desires.

We need to understand that we entered this marriage expecting more out of each other than God does. We wanted our spouse to always be in a good mood, make no mistakes of their own but always be understanding when we mess up, never display their anger or frustration while being forever considerate of our feelings, and listen to us complain for hours at a time without being negative or critical toward us. In short, we expected perfection out of our spouse while wanting them to bear with us in our imperfections. This results in us casting blame on each other for every problem, seldom acknowledging our own faults. It is only when we accept the fact that more of the problem lies in our expectations and not in our spouse's failures that we will begin to make progress.

There is no greater freedom in marriage than the **Freedom To Fail**. There is no greater pressure in marriage than the absence of that freedom. Living in a relationship where there is no room for failure is like living in a prison. It is a suffocating, stifling, overwhelming responsibility to always be perfect in every way. This expectation of perfection does not even need to be spoken, it just needs to be implied. When one or both spouses live under the assumption that any one mistake could lead to belittling, retribution, or unwarranted threats, tension replaces any possibility of comfort or connection, and a wedge separates the couple. The freedom to fail allows us to reach for new heights and strive for a deeper relationship, but without it we won't even try or take any chances for fear that our efforts will fall short and we will ultimately pay the price. Most of the greatest inventions in the world were discovered after a series of failures. Creative inventors never see unsuccessful attempts as failure, but learn from each one and pursue their goals. The only true failure is the failure to try.

God gives us the freedom to fail, and even sent His own Son to pay for those failures. He expects us to strive for perfection, but acknowledges that we will not reach it this side of eternity. He does not give us free reign to sin, nor does He allow us to make excuses for wrong behavior, but He does give us room to be human. We need to make the same allowance for each other. It is in our failure that we learn and grow, becoming more the person and spouse that we need to be.

Admission of Fault

Admitting that we are wrong and that our spouse is right is one of the hardest things we ever learn to do in marriage. It is also one of the most important. The more natural thing to do is shift the blame, point fingers, make excuses, and deny responsibility. Admitting that we are at fault means that we also need to change. It means that we are accepting responsibility for our own actions and owning up to our own mistakes. It is making the effort to see our own sinful nature as readily as we see our spouse's.

The first step in admitting our fault is the **Confession Of Sin**. To confess means that we admit that we are wrong, that we agree that our behavior is unacceptable. We need to confess to ourselves, to our God, and to our spouse. If we don't admit to ourselves that we are wrong we will never confess those wrongs to God or to our spouse. It is also important that we understand what we are confessing is sin. It is not a difference of opinion. It is not a wrong choice. It is not a slip up or a mistake. Sin is anything that falls short of what God wants for us, anything that is contrary to His will. It literally means "missing the mark." It is easy for us all to minimize the seriousness of our sin, making excuses for ourselves and justifying our attitude and behavior.

Confession involves a broken heart, a change in spirit. When we confess our sins we must be specific. "I don't know what I did wrong, but I'm sorry," is not confession. We go to God seeking forgiveness for specific actions and attitudes that are in direct opposition to His will. We go to our spouse asking forgiveness for specific things we have done that have hurt them. This attitude of confession not only applies to our marriage, but also to our relationship with our children. If we can't confess to our God who is above us, and we can't confess to our spouse who is our equal, we will never be able to confess to our children who are under our authority.

Paul Moody, the son of evangelist Dwight Moody, tells a story about his father that illustrates this point. He says that one day a family friend was visiting in their home, and because it was past his bedtime Paul's dad asked him to go to bed. Not meaning to be disobedient, he thought his dad was asking him to go to his room as soon as the family friend left. A few minutes later Dwight Moody spoke to his son one more time, this time with some anger in his voice. Paul Moody writes:

> This time I retreated immediately and in tears, for it was an almost unheard-of thing that he should speak with such directness or give an order unaccompanied by a smile. But I had barely gotten into my little bed before he was kneeling beside it in tears and seeking my forgiveness for having spoken so harshly .... Half a century must have passed since then, and while it is not the earliest of my recollections I think it is the most vivid, and I can still see that room in twilight and that large bearded figure with the great shoulders bowed above me, and hear the broken voice and the tenderness in it. Before then and after, I saw him holding the attention of thousands of people, but asking the forgiveness of his unconsciously disobedient little boy for having spoken harshly seemed to me then and seems now a finer and greater thing, and to it I owe more than I owe to any of his sermons. For to this I am indebted for an understanding of the

meaning of the Fatherhood of God, and a belief in the love of God had its beginnings that night in my childish mind.[1]

I can never read that story without crying. I think of all the times I have spoken harshly to my children or corrected them in my anger, and it breaks my heart. My goal as a parent is that my children can have memories of me like Paul Moody has of his father. I want to be a man who runs to my wife admitting my wrongdoing and seeking her forgiveness. I want my kids to see that. I want to be a dad who is never too prideful to fall on my knees in front of my children and tell them I am sorry, seeking their forgiveness, and restoring a right relationship. I want to be a child of God who regularly falls before my God, confessing my sins, and asking Him to not only forgive me but change me as well.

James 5:16 says that we are to confess our sins to each other "so that you may be healed." Those are powerful words. Many marriages today are hurting, even dying, because they are lacking this aspect of confession. When couples learn to admit their sinful ways to each other, and seek forgiveness, and make an effort at restoring the relationship, God says that then they can be healed. This is a part of God's plan for marriage that I believe is absent, even in many Christian couples.

Another aspect of admitting my fault is the **Acknowledgment Of Hurt**. We all know that the famous movie line, "love means never having to say you're sorry," is a lie, but we must also remember that just saying those words is not enough, it's too easy. We can use the words "I'm sorry" as the bandage that covers every wound. If we say those two little words we expect the other person to forgive us, then and there. After all, we did our part, right? No! We say things like, "I said I was sorry, now what else do you want?" or "That's not what I meant, so if you took it that way that is your problem." Those words make no concession for the hurt that we caused the one we love. They belittle the other person for their feelings, or blame them for not understanding what we meant. The fact is, the result of our communication is what counts, not the intent. When we hurt someone, especially our spouse, our heart needs to break instead of our back going up. Sometimes we act like our words or our actions are no big deal, when in fact hurt feeling are a big deal. We must acknowledge them, and then do something about it.

Another problem many of us have is seen in our expectation that the matter can be resolved quickly. Hurt feelings sometimes take a while to heal. Asking forgiveness does not make the pain go away. Our spouse may choose to forgive us, but they still have to

work through their feelings. I do not believe in the saying that "time heals all wounds," but I do believe that all wounds take a little time to heal. We need to be willing to allow for that time.

Sometimes when the hurt is deep we need to make **Compensation For Pain**. I want to make sure that I am clear on this point. I am not saying that we can buy our way out of trouble. I am not saying that we patronize our spouse with a cheap effort at excusing our behavior. Nor am I saying that begging or groveling will make the pain go away. What I am saying is that sometimes mere words are not enough, they need to be accompanied by action. There is nothing wrong with expressing our sorrow in tangible ways like cards, flowers, or an evening out. The biggest thing we can do to make up for the pain we have caused is to change our ways, to make sure that we never repeat that harmful behavior or attitude again. We need to work hard to show our spouse that we truly are sorry for hurting them, and that our heart is broken for causing them such pain. Luke 19:8 talks about what we need to do if we have cheated anyone out of anything. This verse says that we should pay them back, make restitution for what we have taken. I believe that verse could apply to emotional issues as well as possessions. If we have robbed our spouse of joy or peace or comfort or security then we need to work at restoring those feelings in a practical way.

Allowance of Forgiveness

Two things must be present in order for a marriage to be successful: Genuine brokenness and genuine forgiveness. One without the other will not be enough to sustain it. When we admit our faults to each other the words must be accompanied by a true

broken heart suffered over the pain we have caused. Our spouse needs to see that we are hurting deeply because we have hurt them deeply. Anything short of this is nothing more than shallow words aimed at getting oneself out of trouble. Genuine forgiveness must also be present. Once our spouse has offered a heartfelt, sincere apology, we must begin the hard work of genuine forgiveness. Without it our marriage will stay mired in the deep waters of pain with no chance of survival.

What is forgiveness? "It is the art of healing inner wounds inflicted by other people's wrongs."[2] It is "the willingness to let go of self-harming or ineffective forms of anger, choosing instead to turn over ultimate resolution of the wrong to God."[3] Arch Hart, when speaking to a group of lay counselors, said that forgiveness is "surrendering your felt right to get even." In offering this type of forgiveness we can begin the process of healing that is necessary for the reconciliation of our relationship.

We need to remember that **The Aim Is Not To Blame**. I can tell my wife that I have forgiven her, but if I remind her of her wrongdoing on a regular basis, continuously bringing it back up and blaming her for the damage she has done, then I have not really forgiven her. Colossians 3:13 says that we must forgive each other as the Lord has forgiven us. That forgiveness is unconditional, complete, heartfelt and real. There is no limit to His forgiveness. He forgives the little things and He forgives the big things. Getting even is natural, but forgiving is not, it is supernatural. We want to do it His way, and in order to do so we need His help.

Have you ever said something like this: "I forgive you, but. . .?" "I forgive you, but you had better not do that again." "I forgive you, but you owe me." "I forgive you, but I am never going to let you forget this one." Those kind of statements do not reflect genuine forgiveness. Any apology or offer of forgiveness that is followed by the word "but" is automatically negated. Those three little letters erase every word preceding them. Real forgiveness is "I forgive you" period. It means that the issue is over. Granted, the pain from that issue may last for a long time, and healing from that pain is a process, but the issue itself needs to be buried.

If we have been wronged by our spouse, it is normal to feel hurt, and our offer of forgiveness is not excusing their behavior. However, sometimes our blaming stems more from our skewered perspective than it does genuine wrongdoing. We need to make sure that forgiveness is warranted and that our take on the whole matter is accurate. "Unfair blame tends to be accompanied by black-and-white thinking, no gray. No room is allowed for any explanation or insight regarding the wrong deed. Straight thinking, on the other hand, will take into account the many factors involved in wrong deeds while also labeling wrong to be exactly what it is - wrong."[4]

We also need to understand The **Danger Of Anger.** Ephesians 4:31 says that we need to "get rid of all bitterness, rage and anger, brawling and slander, along with every form of malice." That verse sounds like a description of some marriages I know. All anger is not bad. Anger is a God-given emotion, an emotion that Christ possessed and expressed during His time on earth. It is not a matter of us never feeling or displaying our anger, instead it is an issue of making sure that those feelings and actions are honoring to Christ. Controlled anger is not only healthy, it is necessary. That emotion can motivate us toward action or it can protect us from danger. We just want to learn to deal with it in the right way.

Neil Clark Warren describes four wrong ways to deal with anger:

- If you pretend you have no anger and try to bury it, it can bury you - literally - by triggering a heart attack or stroke.
- If you let it out in the wrong way, it can ruin your marriage, alienate your children, or get you fired.
- If you somehow turn it around on yourself, it can tear your self-image apart, destroy your self-esteem, and set you up for all kinds of psychic pain.
- If you fail to process it when you experience it, it may turn

to resentment; and if it does, you can become hostile, negative, and impossible to be around.[5]

We will never be capable of developing and maturing loving feelings for our spouse if our heart is full of bitterness, anger, and hatred. We have to let go of the one if we want to gain the other. It is like the oil in a car. It is impossible to add clean oil until we first drain out the old. We need to drain our hearts of the unwillingness to forgive, and allow God to replace that with a new ability and desire to make a fresh start.

In the midst of this discussion on confession we cannot forget about **The Freedom In Forgiveness**. When we refuse to forgive we allow the pain to continue, and allow the other person to keep hurting us. We forgive because we have been commanded to, because the other person needs our forgiveness, and because we need to let go of the unforgiveness that imprisons us. We find true freedom when we choose to forgive others and when others willingly forgive us. So it is not only for their sake that we forgive, but for our own as well. It is important to remember that although it takes two to reconcile, it only takes one to forgive. Even if the other person doesn't ask for forgiveness, or even admit that they were wrong, we can still choose to forgive. It is not something we have to feel, it is something we have to do.

Some people come to me frustrated saying, "John, I know that I am supposed to forgive and forget, but I just can't seem to let it go." Here is my question: Who says that we are supposed to forgive and forget? Did Jesus? Is it even in the Bible? No! God never told us to forgive and forget because He knows that is physically impossible for us. Our brains are the ultimate computers, storing everything for later retrieval. The Biblical command is not "forgive and forget," it is "forgive and forgive and forgive and forgive ...." Every time we remember and feel that pain we are to stop and tell the Lord that today we choose to forgive that person all over again.

Forgiveness is hard, but it is not impossible. While hanging on the cross Jesus forgave those who were crucifying Him. While we were still sinners He died for us, to offer us complete forgiveness. No matter what we do or how much we mess up, we can never out sin His forgiveness. We need to live out that truth in our marriage. When we hurt each other we need to seek forgiveness, and when we have been hurt we need to offer it. Whoever said "confession is good for the soul" knew what they were talking about.

Chapter 7

CLOSENESS

In Chapter 1 I talked about marriage as a triangle, a relationship between husband, wife, and God. The closer the husband and wife get to God, the closer they automatically are drawn to each other. Marriage is like a triangle in another way. A complete, full, satisfying marital relationship is made up of three distinct aspects: Commitment, Intimacy, and Passion.[1] Commitment is the glue that holds the couple together, the promise to work through every issue, the vow that divorce is not an option. When I speak of intimacy here I am talking about the emotional connection, the friendship and closeness that is shared between two soul mates. Physical passion is also an important part of this marriage triangle, a part that God designed and gave us as a beautiful gift to be shared. Seldom is there a time in marriage when all three of these aspects are equally strong. Sometimes our commitment is unwavering and our friendship is growing, but because of our stage of life the passion has waned a little. There are other times when the physical aspect of our marriage has never been better, but other struggles lead to doubts and frustrations that cause our commitment level to weaken. Busyness, small children, and financial pressures can drive a wedge into our relationship, leaving us feeling emotionally cold and distant. The goal is to be constantly working on all three areas of importance, never allowing any one of them to completely disappear. Marriage is a lifetime of hard work striving to find a healthy balance in these three areas. It is God's desire that we have a marriage built upon a solid commitment -- spiritual intimacy, one in which there is a genuine connection -- emotional intimacy, and one that develops and cherishes sexual closeness -- physical intimacy.

Spiritual Intimacy

The commitment, the foundation of a marriage, is based on a spiritual depth, a closeness that develops in a couple as a result of both individuals growing closer to the Lord. This type of intimacy is difficult to achieve, even for the most committed Christian couple, for a variety of reasons. Several years ago I attended a counseling conference in which author, speaker, and president of The American Association Of Christian Counselors, Tim Clinton, spoke about the barriers to spiritual intimacy. He listed time, children, church, personality, education, preoccupation, ignorance, fear, anger, pain, and lack of communication among the culprits. I'm sure this is not an exhaustive list, but it does give us a brief picture of the complexity of developing genuine spiritual closeness. He summed up all these issues in five categories: Stress, Satan, Self, Scripts, and Speed. As we attempt to develop the intimacy God has designed for us the stresses of life get in the way. We know that Satan's goal is to steal, kill, and destroy all that God wants to build. Our selfishness is definitely a major barrier, understanding how much easier it is for us all to pursue our own desires rather than placing the desires of our spouse ahead of our own. We don't need to be married for very long to realize how quickly we develop scripts, those same annoying arguments we have over and over again that never get resolved. Even when we are making progress in all of these areas sometimes just the speed of our lives prevents us from getting close. The results are emptiness, distance, loneliness, and an inability to make a genuine spiritual connection.

In order to combat these destructive forces there are several things that we must do. We need to make sure that we are spending **Time In The Word**. The Bible says of itself, "Your Word is a lamp to my feet and a light to my path." (Psalm 119:105). God's Word gives us clear direction and hope for the future. It is important for each of us to spend quality time reading and studying the Bible individually and as a couple. This is not as easy as it sounds. I became a Christian at the age of eight, and as I grew I learned the value of having a personal quiet time with the Lord. When I got married I believed that developing couple time in the Word would be natural and simple. I was wrong. What was natural for me individually was very awkward when I tried to share it with Pamela. Using tools like a couple's devotional Bible helped us make the transition a little smoother. We also learned how valuable it is when we have our personal devotional time and later share the truths we learned with each other. Trying to grow a marriage without turning to God's Word for direction is like trying to build a house without a blueprint. It is foolish, and the end result is undesirable.

We also need to spend **Time With The Church**. Spending time with the church does not necessarily mean spending time at the church. Spending too much time at the church building can be un-healthy for a marriage. Over the years I have seen the church, with all its activities and ministries, become "the other woman" for some men. They begin to find their fulfillment in their service, fulfillment they were not finding at home. They spend more and more time there, avoiding the real issues in their marriage and family. I have listened as many a husband has complained about the enormous amount of time and energy their wife is giving to "the Lord's work", all the while ignoring his needs and the needs of their children. There definitely needs to be a balance.

We know that the church is not a building, it's the people. Spending time worshiping, serving, and fellowshipping with others who are like minded is a healthy habit for Christian couples. These relationships offer accountability, encouragement, support and prayer. Sometimes just hearing other couples share their struggles is an encouragement, a reminder that we are not alone in this jour-ney. We learn from each other and are motivated to work harder at our faith and our marriage. Couples who worship and serve togeth-er strengthen their spiritual connection. Drawing closer to God and ministering to His people side by side, hand in hand, draws us closer to each other as well.

Along with spending time in God's Word and with His people, it is important that we spend **Time On Our Knees**. This means pray-ing for each other and praying with each other on a regular ba-sis. I believe this is the most essential aspect for a couple's spiritual growth, but it is also the most difficult to achieve. As we have seen, statistics say that only 4% of Christian couples pray together.[2] It's a statistic that is not difficult to understand. Satan knows the value and power of prayer. He also desires more than anything else to steal our spiritual intimacy, kill any chance of a close connection, and destroy our relationship. The last thing he wants from a couple is to see them praying together. Not only is prayer something Satan hates, it is also something that is very private and personal. Next to sexual intercourse prayer is the most intimate activity we share as a couple. We are opening ourselves up emotionally and spiritually to God in front of our spouse. That can be very uncomfortable. There is a vulnerability involved that makes us shy away from praying with each other. Even those who have no trouble praying in public, or with total strangers, or having devotions with their children, may still have difficulty opening up to God in front of their spouse.

I rarely see couples in my office who report that they pray together on a nightly basis. That may be a coincidence, or it may mean that if they are talking to God regularly they don't need to come talk to me. Praying together is one of the best deterrents to divorce. In chapter 1 we looked at some statistics from David and Jan Arp. They say that only one out of 1,500 couples who pray together get a divorce.[3] Isn't that amazing! Let's see - one out of two couples in America end their marriage vs one of 1,500 who pray. I think we need to pray! One of the biggest struggles I see in couple counseling is the slow erosion of the relationship over years of bickering and the growing resentment over a multitude of unresolved issues. When a couple comes together each night to hold hands and pray they are essentially erasing the slate. They are going together to the throne of grace asking God to help them forgive each other

and strive to do better in their relationship. Each day they are start-
ing new instead of building upon the hurts and disappointments of
the days before.

As we draw closer to the Lord together in prayer every aspect
of our relationship should get better. Regular prayer should open up
lines of communication. It breaks down walls and helps us resolve
conflict. Prayer forces a couple to resolve their issues. It is extremely
difficult to continue arguing with each other if you are laying all
those issues before the Lord. Seeking Him together on behalf of
our children will give us strength and direction as to how we should
raise them. Difficult decisions are made with His guidance, and our
friendship will grow as we spend more time together in His presence.
Prayer together can even improve our sex lives:

> Sociologist Andrew Greely surveyed married people and
> found that the happiest couples were those who pray to-
> gether. Couples who frequently pray together are twice as
> likely as those who pray less often to describe their marriage
> as being highly romantic. They also report higher sexual
> satisfaction and more sexual ecstacy! As strange as it may
> sound, there is a strong link in marriage between prayer and
> sex. For one thing, frequency of prayer is a more powerful
> predictor of marital satisfaction that frequency of sexual
> intimacy. But get this: Married couples who pray together
> are ninety percent more likely to report higher satisfaction
> with their sex life than couples who do not pray together.
> Also, women who pray with their partner tend to be more
> orgasmic. That doesn't sound right, does it? After all, mar-
> ried churchgoers are painted by the media as prudes who

think sex is dirty. Well, let the media say what they want, but prayerful couples know better.[4]

Why should these facts surprise us? Doesn't it make sense that when we do marriage the way God designed it that every aspect would be better? God created sex. When we allow Him to be an active part of our sex life it should get better. God designed marriage. When we give our marriage over to Him daily it should not surprise us that He will mold it into what He wants it to be.

Emotional Intimacy

The Biblical principle of "the two shall become one" is all about intimacy. It includes the act of sexual intercourse, but it is so much deeper than that. This connection, this oneness, is a God-given need inside every human heart. This is especially true for women, but men need it as well. In spite of their own need for it this can be difficult for men to understand, and even harder for them to display. Many of us like to talk about our spouse being our very best friend, but few of us ever reach that level of emotional intimacy. More and more couples I talk to describe their marital relationship as being more like room mates than soul mates. This is not God's plan. In one of my classes at Fuller Theological Seminary, professors Jack and Judy Balswick helped me understand some basic needs all of us have and the importance of getting them met.[5]

Inside every person there is a deep abiding need **To Know And Be Known.** In the book of Genesis the Bible says that Adam "knew" his wife. Again, although referring in part to the sexual connection, this "knowing" implies a closeness in heart and soul. It is God's desire that husband and wife know each other better than they know anyone else, maybe even better than they know themselves. Marriage should be an open book, one of complete honesty and vulnerability. True honesty in marriage means that we tell the truth, the whole truth, and nothing but the truth. There is no room for secrets or lies, no place for hidden agendas or ulterior motives. It is not a relationship where we hide emotionally from each other, where fear and anxiety are worn as a mask to cover overprotective hearts.

In counseling I see many relationships in pain and hear a lot of emptiness and hurt expressed through broken hearts from unfulfilled dreams and expectations. The pain is deep and real, and the gap that has been forged between the husband and wife is so wide that the idea of healing seems distant, if possible at all. One of the comments that hurts my heart the most is when I hear someone say of their spouse, "I don't even know them anymore." This most basic of all needs to know and be known has ceased to be met, and the result is loneliness and helplessness. That emotional knowledge and connection is hard to explain when it is present, but it is painfully evident when it has gone.

A second need found deep within every human heart is the need **To Love And Be Loved**. We are created by love and for love, and without it we will never experience real life. We all know that love is not a feeling, it is a choice. Feelings are thankfully involved, but they do not determine our actions. When we allow our feelings to dictate our actions we are in deep trouble, because those feelings are fickle, they come and they go. We choose to give our love to our spouse when the loving feelings are overflowing from our hearts and when they are completely absent. That commitment, that promise, that we will continue to love each other no matter what is foundational to marriage. The Bible says that we are to love each other as Christ loves the church. His love is unconditional and never ending. That is what we are to be fleshing out in our marital relationship.

When as a couple we find ourselves making comments such as, "the love I once had for her is gone," or "I just don't love him anymore," we can either look at this as a reason to quit the marriage, or we can see it as a God-sized challenge to learn the real meaning of love and motivate ourselves to recommit to that love and rediscover that deep connection. Marriage should be a solid bond, a "whatever it takes" promise that breathes hope and security into each partner. It is the comfort of knowing that in the good times and in the bad times neither of us is going anywhere. That is our vow. That is love.

A final need embedded in every heart is the need **To Give And Be Given**. There is no greater joy than that of giving to others. It is meaningful and satisfying in a way that can never be matched by any amount of receiving. As we strive to live a life that models Jesus, self-sacrifice is a requirement. Jesus said that He did not come to be served but to serve others. Marriage provides a great avenue to live out this Christ-like characteristic. In a Christ-centered marriage both husband and wife should find themselves constantly tripping over each other trying to out give the other. The Scripture tells us that we should always view each other's needs as more important than our own. When both partners embrace this value the marriage will thrive.

The problem is found in the fact that each partner is a sinful, self-ish person, who, when push comes to shove, wants their own needs met. We are afraid to set aside our own desires and concentrate on those of our spouse for fear that our desires will fall by the way side, and will never be met. When I discuss this principle with couples I hear some reoccurring concerns: "So what you are saying to me John is that I should just become a doormat, letting him walk all over me." "John, if I don't stand up for my own needs and desires no one ever will." So, you want me to become a wimpy husband, jumping to attention at her every whim." The answer to those objections is a resounding no! A marriage made up of two people who are ve-hemently pursuing their own agendas, with neither one willing to budge, is a disaster. But a marriage where one person always dom-inates the other is no better. The answer is for both partners to set aside their selfishness and give sacrificially to each other. Marriage is to be a two-way street.

When couples buy into this idea and first begin to implement these principles usually the same thing occurs. The couple will come back a few weeks later, and when asked to share how things are going I get a response like this: "Well, it was going pretty good. We were really trying. He genuinely seemed to care about me, and he was lovingly putting my needs first. And I was doing the same. But about a week into it he must have gotten up on the wrong side of the bed or something, because he was mean and selfish and hurt-ful. So I told him that if he wasn't going to try, neither was I. So here we are, right back where we started." And therein lies the problem. We are usually willing to try putting our spouse's needs ahead of our own as long as they are equal to the task. It becomes a 50/50 relationship. "You do your part and I'll do mine. You give to me and I'll give to you, but if you slack off, don't count on me to be the only one giving. I'm not going to be made a fool of." Is it really selflessness if my actions depend on yours? Is it Christ-like behavior if I quit as soon as you flinch?

Several years ago I was counseling a couple who were both bound and determined not to give an inch. They kept a tally of each other's rights and wrongs, and were in no way going to allow the scales to become unbalanced. One day as I was discussing this principle of putting your spouse's needs ahead of your own, he looked me square in the eyes and said, "Yea John, but am I supposed to just keep giving and giving when she is giving nothing in return? Isn't there a limit?" I looked down and saw a WWJD bracelet around his wrist, and I said to him, "Well, what would Jesus do? I mean I guess you wear that bracelet because that's the way you want to live. So, did Jesus give and give and then reach a certain point and say, 'This isn't fair. I am not giving anything else until these people meet me half way.' I don't think so. He gave and gave and gave until He had nothing left to give. He gave His very life. And you see, Jesus asks us to love our wives the way He loves us. In answer to your question, the answer is no. There is no limit." He didn't have much of a response.

We all need to give and we all need to receive. God, in His infinite wisdom, has given us the institution of marriage as a way to get both of those needs met. As long as both partners are focused on their own needs neither one of their needs will get met. But when both give sacrificially to each other, giving all of their effort to meeting the other's needs, all of their needs will be satisfied. John Kennedy once said, "Ask not what your country can do for you. Ask what you can do for your country." We can apply that same principle to marriage. "Ask not what your spouse can do for you. Ask what you can do for your spouse."

Physical Intimacy

Physical intimacy and emotional intimacy go hand in hand. The more one grows the more the other grows. The problem is that this emotional and physical intimacy are seen in a completely different light by husband and wife. For most women, their level of emotional connection determines their level of physical desire. Whereas most men's level of emotional closeness is controlled by their level of physical satisfaction. For example, a woman whose husband is kind and caring and keenly aware of her emotional needs, meeting them with regularity, is more open to his sexual advances. However, a husband whose wife is consistently satisfying his sexual desires will be more attentive to her emotional needs. It is easier for a woman to open herself up sexually if she feels secure and loved. A man who is content sexually will find that he is thinking more and more about his wife, and as a result he might call her more often, or send her a card, or just give her a hug for no reason. I know that I am speaking in generalities, but I find this cycle to be true. A wife complains to me that she would be more desirous of her husband if he would put just a little bit of effort into their relationship, making her feel loved and special. Her husband tells me that he would find it easier to put forth emotional effort if she would show any desire for him sexually.

Who's right and who's wrong? Nobody. Both. Either way they are stuck, waiting on the other to go first. If neither of them decides to change things, refusing to get the cycle spinning in the other direction, they will find themselves empty and bitter and resentful.

Our physical intimacy involves several issues. The first is **The Issue Of Purity**. Hebrews 13:4 says, "Marriage should be honored by all, and the marriage bed kept pure, for God will judge the adulterer and all the sexually immoral." Marital sexual purity obviously means that we commit ourselves only to each other, never allowing anyone else access into our relationship. Physical and emotional affairs poison the marriage and can take years of exhausting effort to overcome, if they are overcome at all. There is no room for "harmless flirting," which is an oxymoron, or close intimate friendships with the opposite sex. We steadfastly defend our relationship from any one or any thing that could bring it harm. Faithfulness breeds freedom. If we want sexual freedom within the marriage, we must maintain sexual faithfulness within the marriage.

For some marriages the issue of purity has less to do with outside influences than it does with what goes on inside the privacy of our own homes. What impure things are we bringing to bed with us? We have talked some already about the problem of pornography, but it must be addressed again. If we as Christian couples think that we can bring the images found on the internet, in the magazines, in the raunchy romance novels, or on the movies and late night cable channels, into our heads and into our beds without any harm being done, we are sadly mistaken. Those images are a distortion of God's sexual creation. They will confuse our desires, create unrealistic expectations, disturb our thought lives, and warp our view of marital sex. We must even be careful of the influence of prime time T.V. The moral standards are changing daily, and what used to be normal for an R-rated movie is now regularly seen on network television. We must guard the purity of our marriage. (I try to do my part by turning off that other trash and watching more and more sporting events. I know it's a sacrifice, but I'll do whatever's best for my marriage!)

Another area to be addressed is **The Issue Of Privacy**. Married love and sex is very private, not even to be talked about outside of marriage. What I mean here is not sharing the sexual details of our marriage with anyone else. If we do so we are giving away something that belongs solely to the two of us, essentially "casting our pearls before swine." What goes on behind closed doors should stay there. The Bible says in Proverbs 20:19 that "a gossip betrays a confidence; so avoid a man who talks too much." I believe this is certainly applicable when it comes to marital sex. The point is that it is nobody else's business.

Men get a bad rap when it comes to this topic, but I don't know how true I find that to be. My wife says that when a group of women get together and the topic of sex comes up, ladies like to talk. I can't recall very many occasions with my friends when this was the topic of conversation. What I do think is true is that single guys like to talk about their sex lives more than single women, and married women like to discuss their sex lives more than married men. Either way it is wrong and unhealthy. And if we find ourselves around a couple who is continually making sexual comments or innuendos, or discussing the details of their private lives, we need to be careful.

They are dangerous. Their unhealthy preoccupation usually reveals some insecurity and probably some unhappiness. They are sharing those details for a reason. Either they find it exciting sharing titillating details with others, or they are sending out vibes that they are looking for something more. If they have to talk about their sex life all the time it probably means that it is not nearly as good as they make it out to be.

We need to understand that privacy breeds intimacy. When we communicate to each other a deep respect for the beautiful gift of sexual closeness God has given us, we create a green house effect for intimacy. Our sex life is given the opportunity to grow in the safe environment of a closed and protected relationship. Couples need to talk to each other more about their intimate needs and desires, and stop talking to outside influences. With each other we need to be open and vulnerable and free, but in front of others modesty and privacy must be our guides.

When it comes to the topic of physical intimacy what probably interests us the most is **The Issue Of Pleasure**. God created sex to be something enjoyable for both husband and wife. It should be something we look forward to, not dread. If that aspect of our lovemaking is absent then there is a problem that needs to be addressed. When speaking of the sexual relationship one has with his wife Proverbs 5:19 says, "A loving doe, a graceful deer - may her breasts satisfy you always, may you be ever captivated by her love." I love that phrase - ever captivated. It implies such connection, such a oneness. That is what the sexual aspect of our relationship should

bring. After all, sex is the only thing that husband and wife share together that they can't share with anyone else. It is their unique gift.

Too many times we act embarrassed when discussing what God
was not embarrassed to create. Throughout His Word He is clear
that sexual intimacy is His gift to the marriage, something that He
sees as beautiful. In the Song of Solomon, the king's wife declares
that she delights in bringing him pleasure and "filling his cup." She
calls her sexual favors "lilies," and tells of how she loves to give them
to her husband. God is for sex. Our problem is that we either gravi-
tate to the extreme of seeing our sexuality as shameful, or we go to
the other extreme of exploiting and corrupting it.

Finally we want to look at **The Issue Of Power**. God never intended our sexual intimacy to be used in a power struggle, and yet
sometimes that's what it becomes. We take something God created and intended for pleasure and use it to manipulate and guilt
each other. Ladies, it is ungodly behavior when you use sex as a tool
to get what you want. Instead of giving yourself to your husband
out of love and desire, you hold out on your sexual relationship, ma-
nipulating him for your own selfish desires, letting him know that he
will get what he wants when you get what you want. Men, we too
can take what God has given us and twist it around for our own
pleasure. Instead of respecting our wives and building an emotional
connection that allows them to freely give to us, we try to guilt them
into sex by misquoting Scripture, holding their "responsibility to submit" over their heads.

1 Corinthians 7:3 tells us to fulfill our marital duties to each other. This is God's plan for our lives, drawing us closer to each other

and meeting our needs so that we won't be tempted to stumble. We should fulfill each other's sexual needs out of love, desire, and selflessness. We must also respect each other in those times when they don't want to be physically intimate. When it comes to this topic of power there are two forms of sexual selfishness. One extreme is when we <u>keep our body from our spouse</u>. The Bible says that our bodies belong to each other. Continually refusing to give our body to our spouse is ignoring that teaching. The other extreme is when we <u>force our body on our spouse</u>. The Bible also teaches us to put each other's needs ahead of our own. When we ignore our spouse's need by demanding from them what they are not ready to give, we are being selfish and hurtful. Sex within marriage cannot be forced or demanded. In the Song of Solomon the kings lover declares that, "my own vineyard is mine to give." Again, the key here is pleasure not pressure. If both partners willingly give then both partners lovingly receive.

Chapter 8

CLEAVING

"For this reason a man will leave his father and mother and be united to his wife, and they will become one flesh" (Genesis 2:24). This is a powerful verse that is quoted often in wedding ceremonies, but the main point is missed in many marriages. Much of our focus is on what it means to be one flesh, but we sometimes skip over the part about leaving family and being united in marriage. The oneness cannot be attained if there has not been a healthy break from the family of origin. Many marriages suffer because of this issue. What does it really mean to leave and cleave?

The Process of Leaving

Let me make one point perfectly clear, there can be no cleaving without first leaving. Leaving entails so much more than just the physical. A woman can move thousands of miles away from her parents and yet still be overly connected emotionally. A man can begin his new life with his new wife far away from his family of origin, while still being 100% present with them in his heart. We've all heard about the apron strings, but we may not realize how far those strings can stretch. We need to understand the familial pattern or concept in which we were raised. My concept of family closeness might be very different from that of my new bride. A lack of under-standing this issue along with unrealistic expectations can lead to a lot of pain and confusion. In this chapter I want to look at three different types of families: Enmeshed, Disengaged, and Differentiat-ed. (Much of this material was gleaned from lectures by Jack and Judy Balswick).[1]

First let's look at the **Enmeshed** family. This type family is so fused together that there is no healthy separateness. It's hard to tell where one person stops and the other person begins. There's a confusing overlap of each family member that makes them too close, over-in-volved, and over-controlling. In this family everybody is in everybody else's business - always. Conflict within an enmeshed family will sel-dom involve just two people. The conflict spreads until every other family member is triangled, or drawn in. A young couple will struggle forming a new committed relationship because one or both of the parties can't break from their family of origin. The new spouse has a difficult time gaining access into the inner circle. He/she feels like an outsider, even though they married into the family.

If the last person you talk to at night before you drift off to sleep is your mother - you are enmeshed. If every time you have an ar-gument you pick up the phone and ask dad his opinion - you are enmeshed. If you can't go out to eat without first calling up your parents to invite them - you are enmeshed. If you took your par-ents on your honeymoon - you are enmeshed! This type family is unhealthy, allowing no room for individuality. It is also unnatural for a family to be this connected, and it is unbiblical according to the Genesis 2 passage.

Second, let's take a look at the **Disengaged** family. This family is marked by emotional distance. There is no personal interaction, no free give and take. There is an unhealthy amount of space between family members. There are definitely boundaries, but those boundaries are too thick, too closed off. In the enmeshed family there is no healthy separateness. In the disengaged family there is no healthy connectedness. A young couple where one or both parties come from disengaged families will have a difficult time forming a deep connection, an emotional bond, because they never experienced one growing up. Conflict is a major problem for disengaged people as well. Instead of dealing with it in a healthy way, they usually just ignore it in hopes that it will disappear.

If you can't remember the last time you spoke to your parents - you are disengaged. If three years seems like a good cooling off period after a disagreement - you are disengaged. If family funerals are the only time you see each other - you are disengaged. If your children see pictures of their grandparents and ask who they are - you are disengaged! This family is also unhealthy, making no attempt at creating relational connection. It is unnatural for a family to put such distance between each other, and also unbiblical according to passages that teach us to love and honor our parents.

The enmeshed family's concept of independence is that it is wrong and selfish. They believe that the parents are to retain their place of authority and importance. And while it is true that no matter how old we become we must continue to honor our parents, the enmeshed family believes that obedience to parents is still a priority. The disengaged family's idea of independence is that there must be a complete break from the family of origin. They define family in the strictest context of husband, wife, and children. They rightly understand that obedience to their parents is no longer a responsibility, but they fail to acknowledge the continual obligation to honor. Imagine what it must be like if a person raised in an enmeshed family marries a person raised in a disengaged family. It's okay to be different, just not polar extremes. If so, there will probably be a few issues to be discussed. It is also important to note that from the same family can come one child who adopts and repeats the style he grew up with while another child completely rejects that style and completely adopts the opposite.

These two extreme types of family personality are illustrated in Jesus' parable of the prodigal son (Luke 15:11-32). In this story a father has two sons. The youngest of the two asks for his share of the father's inheritance and runs off to a distant land. There he spends his new found wealth on wild and immoral living, never giving his family a second thought. He is completely disengaged from his father and brother, focusing all of his attention on himself. He ultimately comes to his senses and returns home to his father, prepared to become a slave, assuming that he has lost his right to sonship. When he returns he is greeted with love and acceptance from his father, and welcomed back into the family. His view of family is distorted, but his father's is healthy and balanced.

The oldest son is indignant that his father would be so willing to forgive this ingrate brother of his, who showed complete disrespect and utter disregard for his family. The whole time his brother was in the distant land, he was right where he was supposed to be, with his father. He feels betrayed by the love his father is showering on the black sheep of the family, seeing it as a betrayal of his devotion. He believes that his father owes him complete loyalty because of his faithfulness through the years. The way he understands his relationship with his father is enmeshed and unhealthy, completely self-centered and childish. The father, however, recognizes and acknowledges this son's obedience, and assures him that he will be rewarded, while at the same time celebrating the return of the prodigal son.

This is the goal, to have a **Differentiated** family. This family is represented by a healthy balance. It consists of members who belong and are connected, yet who are also separate and independent. The foundation of this family is mutual love, respect, and acceptance. In the differentiated family parents love their grown children and enjoy spending time with them, while at the same time encourage them to build new lives with their spouse and children. Each family member knows they are always there for each other, but they have individual lives separate from the family of origin. Love, honor, and respect are always present, but the number one obligation shifts to this brand new family unit. This new familial bond cannot be formed if either partner is still caught up in either of these unhealthy patterns.

The Process of Cleaving

The Genesis passage describes two people becoming one flesh. Although this certainly involves the physical, sexual union, it entails so much more. This "one flesh" idea is a picture of two healthy, whole, open people blending together in body, soul, and spirit. A strong connection is formed, stronger than the bond between parent and child. This new bond forms the basis for a brand new family of origin, one that this couple begins. This family unit will one day be affected by children leaving and cleaving to someone new. And the beautiful process continues.

Cleaving to one another means that we **Hold On** to each other. A brand new dependence is formed as we learn to lean on each other for strength and connection. No longer are we dependent on our parents financially, emotionally, or socially. That does not mean that as we are beginning this new life together we cannot accept any help from our family of origin. There may be hard times when we need to turn to our parents for some assistance, but that must be the exception, not the rule. Remember, we left home and are cleaving to each other now. This relationship will not be healthy if we are constantly running back to mom and dad every time we hit a bump in the road.

This dependence we have on each other is a mutual dependence, not a total dependence. We still maintain our individuality. Too many times I hear people talk about finding someone to "complete" them, as if they are only half a person without their partner. The idea is that they are completely incapable of standing on their own. The truth is that when two incomplete people get married they have an incomplete marriage. On the other hand, sometimes I hear married people tell me that they are perfectly fine if their spouse stays or if they leave. This total independence, the idea that life would not change in the least if the marriage dissolved, is unhealthy. Marriage is not supposed to be two completely independent people sharing a house together. The type of dependence I am talking about is when two complete people choose to need each other. Each person has their own identity and individuality, while at the same time form a solid connection that is best described by the term "oneness."

Cleaving also means that we **Hold Together**, that we are unified. As we form this bond with each other there are several enemies to unity that we must recognize. The first enemy is self. It is impossible to cleave to another if we are completely consumed with ourselves. Bonding involves self-giving and the ability to put each other's needs first. Self-centeredness destroys any chance at oneness. A second enemy, if we allow it to become one, is our parents. Even though we are married and are forming a new family unit, sometimes our parents still see us as children. It is important that we defend our spouse, even to their own parents, standing up for them as our partner. We can never allow them to come between us, cause arguments, put our spouse down, or feed the negative. We must also be careful how much we share with them, always mindful of maintaining a healthy family balance. A third possible enemy is our children. We must work hard to never allow our kids to come between us or successfully play us off each other. We work as a team, standing firm and unified. Together we fight these enemies with all of our strength, protecting the unity of our marriage.

Finally, cleaving means that we **Hold Strong** and support each other. Encouragement is a key element necessary for creating and sustaining the marital bond. We can support our spouse by being there for them, building them up when we are alone and in front of others, watching what we say to or about them in front of parents, children, and in-laws, and always putting their feelings ahead of our own. We can't always control our circumstances, but we can control the way we respond to them. When we respond with strength, kindness, and resolution, we confirm our love for each other. Part of holding strong is the promise and assurance that we each are committed to staying together for life - no matter what!

The whole cleaving process is not simple or easy. Forming a solid bond with our spouse takes time and effort. We must keep working hard to gain a mutual dependence on each other, develop unity, and learn how to give loving support to one another. Holding on, holding together, and holding strong are three very difficult tasks. Thankfully we are not left on our own to accomplish them. Ecclesiastes 4:9-12 says:

> Two are better than one, because they have a good return for their work; If one falls down, his friend can lift him up. But pity the man who falls and has no one to help him up! Also, if two lie down together, they will keep warm. But how can one keep warm alone? Though one may be overpowered, two can defend themselves. A cord of three strands is not quickly broken.

When husband and wife cleave to each other they are stronger than either one of them are alone. When God is added to the mix this strand is not easily broken.

The Process of Weaving

My wife is fascinated with the weaving machine. She loves to watch all the individual strands of yarn come together to form a beautiful garment. It is amazing how what looks plain and boring on its on can turn out to be so magnificent when woven together with other seemingly plain strands. The weaving machine gives us a picture of marriage. God takes two individuals and weaves them together to form a beautiful new entity. We all come into this new relationship carrying some memories, some baggage, and plenty of hopes and dreams. The task ahead of us is to sort through the good, the bad, and the ugly, and weave them into a healthy new union. We need to examine our families of origin, determine in our hearts not to repeat some of the destructive patterns, hold on to those aspects that are worth repeating, and form new family memories of our own. Basically we are trying keep the best of what we learned at home and chunk the rest.

Each new family has the responsibility to **Break The Chain** of hurtful family patterns. Habits, sins, lifestyles, addictions, attitudes, behaviors, emotions, language - this is the kind of junk we have to sort through and discard everything we don't want to repeat. Things like name calling, yelling, critical spirit, negativity, uncontrolled temper, prejudice or hatred, lack of affection or encouragement - these are family traits we don't want to perpetuate. We don't have to do things just because our parents did! We cannot use our past as a crutch or excuse for our current behavior and choices. The fact that our father may have never told us that he loved us is not an excuse to be emotionally distant with our own children. Momma's bad temper does not give me free reign to rant and rave. The fact that we might not have been raised in church does not give us a free pass on raising our kids in a spiritual environment. Blaming our parents for our own mistakes and excusing all of our bad habits and poor choices based on our upbringing is a cop out. We must all take responsibility and be held accountable for our own lives. We have a choice as to whether we will break the chain or add another link to it.

I am not suggesting that this is an easy task. Many of these harmful patterns are deeply ingrained in us, and do not just go away because we want them to. Bad habits are hard to break and good habits are hard to make. It may take years of determination and hard work to change unhealthy thinking and sinful behavior. We may need professional help, such as counseling or support groups, but we can find victory. It is wrong to assume that we have no choice but to repeat the mistakes of the past, but it is also a mistake to believe that years and years of bad habits and poor decisions will change over night.

As we take an honest look at our upbringing we will realize that there are some things we enjoyed and want to implement in our new family. Therefore, we have to decide **What To Maintain**. Every family has some positive traits, some good qualities that are worth keeping. Maybe there were some traditions that we grew up with that meant a lot to us, and as a result we want our own kids to experience them as well. We need to look to our parents for anything we saw in them that we admired, respected, loved, or cherished. Some of us have a great heritage that we want to continue. While it is true that we don't have to do things just because our parents did, there are probably some things they did that we will want to repeat.

What is it that we look back on with fond memories? Maybe it was that there was a big emphasis on family. Being able to grow up near grandparents is a privilege in this day and age. If we were able to experience that, it might be a value we desire for our own kids. When Pamela and I began dating I learned that Friday nights were family night. If we went out on Friday it was with her family. At first I found this a little odd, but when I realized that her dad always paid I decided that every date should be on Friday night! When my children began to date I liked that tradition even more. If you grew up having family devotions it is probably ingrained in you. To not implement those nightly prayer times into your new family would be a shame. Maybe it was sports involvement, or music, or church activities, or family game night. Maybe it was just that our parents showed unconditional love. If we look hard enough we will probably find some things worth passing on to the next generation.

It is essential that we break bad habits and it is healthy for us to implement some of our past into our new home, but it is also vitally important that we write **A New Refrain**. A new refrain is what we create with our spouse. We determine what convictions we are going to live by. Together we decide what is fun and unique and special to us. Some things our parents did we will want to repeat and some we will want to break, but we will also want to write our own chapters in the book of our children's lives. As a family we can come up with new ideas, new traditions, new patterns that our children will love and grow up to cherish. What we create today may be repeated for generations to come. What story are we going to write?

We need to understand that when we break some old habits and traditions we may get a little resistance. If we decide that we want to raise our children differently than we were raised, our parents may take that as a slap in the face. They may feel that we are sending a message loud and clear that they did a poor job raising us. It may be as simple as whether you raise your children believing in Santa, the Easter Bunny, and the Tooth Fairy, or it may be as complex as not letting your kids spend the weekend with grandparents unless they promise to bring them to church. While this could be a sticky situation that will require tactful handling, and granted, some things just aren't worth fussing over, the reality is that some battles are worth fighting.

Everyone makes mistakes. Our parents did, we do, and our children will. Part of leaving our parents involves forgiving them for the areas in which they failed. It's like the credit card commercial, "Forgiveness, don't leave home without it." We don't need to excuse our parents for the wrong things they did, we just need to forgive them and move on. That forgiveness needs to be carried into our marriage. We will mess up plenty of times, and we need to forgive each other when we do. We also need to seek forgiveness from our kids when we blow it. One day they will move on to the next phase of their lives, and as they do they will make their own mistakes. We need to be willing to pass on that forgiveness to them, even if they don't ask for it. Our hope is that each generation gets closer to God and closer to figuring out how to do marriage His way.

Chapter 9

CHEATING

Adultery, betrayal, infidelity, affairs, cheating - it doesn't matter what we call it, it is destructive and wrong. We are bombarded with it daily through television, movies, songs, friends, family, politics, even the former President of the United States. None of us have escaped being touched in some way by the pain it leaves behind, and none of us are exempt from the possibility of giving in to its allure. It is such a common topic that we have become immune to it. A few years ago a movie came out called *The Prince Of Tides*. The theme of adultery is so distorted that by the end of the movie those watching it found themselves rooting for the adulterers to get together, and seeing the spouse as the one in the wrong. Satan has a way of twisting the truth so that even believers begin to wonder if leaving their spouse for another person is always the wrong thing to do, or if there might be exceptions. When we begin to see cheating as no big deal for others, we are on a slippery slope. God has a very clear answer for anyone who questions whether sexual faithfulness is right or wrong: "You shall not commit adultery" (Exodus 20:14) As believers we must learn how to filter all of Satan's deception and lies through God's truth of "you shall not." There are no exceptions to the rule. We may choose to disobey God, but we cannot doubt where He stands on the issue. In this chapter I want us to look at four keys to avoiding marital unfaithfulness or betrayal. There are no guarantees, but if we will follow these guidelines our marriages will be stronger, and we will be more likely to stand strong under the enemy's pressure.

Pursue God

When we were first married Pamela worked as a bank teller. The bank would teach them to recognize counterfeit money by having them handle the genuine article. They would get used to the look, feel, and smell of real money, and as a result should be able to easily recognize the counterfeit. That is a good life lesson - the best way to recognize the wrong is to focus on the right. As believers, our goal is to get to know our God as well as we can. We do so by staying in the Word, spending time on our knees, fellowshipping with other believers, and making sure we have accountability in place. The first guideline for us to instill in our lives if we want to remain true to our spouse is to pursue God with all of our heart.

Pursuing God means that we **Commit To His Standards**. Jesus said, "If you love Me, you will obey what I command." (John 14:15) Too many people want to claim a relationship with Christ that is completely void of any obedience. The claims don't match the life-style, and lifestyle is really what it is all about. I believe that we need to understand the difference between morals and ethics. Having strong morals just means that we avoid doing wrong things. Having strong ethics means that we are committed to a lifestyle of avoiding wrong situations. People can maintain morals for a while even though they may be living on the edge of destruction, playing with danger. It is the mentality that says, "I can look as long as I don't touch." An ethical person understands the danger in even looking, the possibility of failure that comes with living too close to the edge. God desires more than just a moral life. He wants us to be guided by holy, ethical principles. His standards run deeper than mere outward behavior, and cut to the very heart of the matter.

God's standards are in place for our protection, not our punishment. The elementary school I attended was on the corner of a busy intersection. Every day we would go out to play for recess. I remember many a day playing kick ball when the ball would roll right up against the fence surrounding the playground. Just on the other side of the fence was the busy street. All of us kids would run full steam to get the ball, even running into the fence if necessary. I have since wondered how we would have approached the situation if the fence had not been in place. I don't believe the ball would have lasted very long, and probably neither would some of us kids. And even if the ball did stop just shy of the street, we would have probably tiptoed up to get it, afraid of getting too close to the traffic. God's fences are like that. They protect us from harm while at the same time freeing us to live within His boundaries.

When I was in my late teens and early twenties I had a good friend named Larry. We liked to hang out, goof off, and drive all over the place. One of our favorite places to go with friends was the mountains. Larry was kind of crazy and had a very fast car - not a good combination. I can remember many times holding on for dear life as we drove way too fast around narrow mountain curves, right up to the edge of the drop off, wheels kicking up gravel. It was scary, but it was also a rush. We were both lucky and survived our immature stupidity. I know too many people who live their lives the exact same way. They like to stay close to the edge, spinning their wheels in the gravel, just barely staying on the road. They are maintaining their morals, but just by the skin of their teeth. The adrenaline rush seems to be worth it, but it only takes one slip and it's all over.

Pursuing God also means that we understand the **Consequences Of Our Sin**. Proverbs 6:31 says, "a man who commits adultery lacks judgment; whoever does so destroys himself." Marital unfaithfulness hurts first and foremost our relationship with God. He is the creator of marriage, and His heart is hurt when we destroy that sacred trust. Obviously our relationship with our spouse is hurt, if not completely destroyed. Marriages can survive betrayal, but it is a long and tedious journey, one that not every spouse is willing to travel. Our children will be crushed. They don't just see it as a marital betrayal, they see it as us betraying them. Their love will probably help them overcome the pain, but they will never again see us through innocent eyes. Our extended family on both sides are hurt by our sinful choice. Our family is embarrassed and our spouse's family becomes angry. All of the friends we share as a couple now feel that they must choose sides. Ultimately most of them will probably fade away out of discomfort and fear, fear that if they continue to hang around the same thing might happen to them.

The ultimate loss is our character, our reputation. The stain is dark and hard to erase. God's grace is sufficient, and He will forgive. What we fail to remember so many times is that just because God forgives our sins does not necessarily mean that He will remove all of the consequences of those sins. Everything does not go back to where it was before just because of a tearful apology, no matter how heartfelt. It will take a long time to rebuild our spouse's trust, even if we both work hard at it. And there is no guarantee that our spouse will be willing to work on it at all. Ultimately adultery could cause us to lose everything that has ever been important to us. Is it worth it?

A final aspect of pursuing God is our willingness to **Cooperate With His Plan**. As believers we have heard it said many times that God has a plan for our life. The question is, do we believe it? If He really does have a plan for each one of us it is important that we seek to understand that plan and follow it will all of our heart. We know that His plan does not include marital betrayal, so if we live by His plan for our life, and not our own, we can be assured that we will remain faithful to our vows. The key is that we stop living to please self and start living to please Him. The problem begins when we start doubting God's provision and look for our own ways to meet our needs. Instead of pursuing Him we begin to pursue our own paths.

Part of God's plan for our life is that He gives us enough strength to stand strong when facing temptation. I Corinthians 10:13 is one of the first verses I ever memorized on my own when I was a young teen. It seemed important to me then, and I know it is important to me now. It says, "No temptation has seized you except what is common to man. And God is faithful; He will not let you be tempted beyond what you can bear. But when you are tempted, He will also provide a way out so that you can stand up under it." Cooperating with His plan involves looking for His way out when we are facing temptation. The Bible promises us that Satan cannot back us into any corner that God has not already created an escape door. Too many times we make the mistake of not only failing to run from temptation, but not even looking around for God's way out.

Cooperating with God's plan for our life means that we are able to sit back and see the big picture, instead of being so caught up in the moment. Adultery takes place when our momentary desires outweigh our long term goals. The principle here is that of delayed gratification. Maturity means that we can put off temporary pleasure now for eternal happiness later. It also means that love and commitment are more important than lust and selfishness.

Pursuing God with all our heart will change our heart, our desires, and our behavior. As we commit our life to following His standards and guidelines, recognizing the severe consequences of our sins, and dedicate our hearts to finding and following His plan for our life, we will strengthen our marital bond and the commitment we made to fidelity. This first key deals with our actions. The second key we will look at deals with our thoughts.

Purify Minds

The Bible says that a man is little more than what he thinks in his heart. Our thoughts lead to our actions which in turn affect our emotions. Understanding this helps us see how important protecting our minds can be. When it comes to the topic of adultery the mind plays a central role. As we will see, affairs begin in our thoughts, long before they ever materialize. James 1:14,15 very clearly lays out **The Process Of Sin**. James says that "each one is tempted when, by his own evil desire, he is dragged away and enticed. Then, after desire has conceived, it gives birth to sin; and sin, when it is full-grown, gives birth to death." There is a distinguishable pattern that is always followed: Desire leads to temptation, temptation leads to conception, conception leads to birth, and birth leads to death.

Notice that the whole sinful process begins with us, our own evil desires. It is not that the devil made us do it, nor is it that the other person deceived and seduced us. The problem began in our own mind. In the damp, dark, depths of our own soul is where sin finds its breeding ground. And it is very subtle. Lustful, adulterous thoughts don't just jump up and down in our mind screaming for us to run out and destroy our marriage. The thoughts begin innocent enough, but slowly grow until they become a monster within us, scratching and fighting to get out. When it gets out it wreaks havoc upon everyone in its path.

We have to understand **The Power Of The Mind.** The things we think about ultimately become the action steps we take. Therefore, we need to be careful and protect our thought life. We know the saying, Garbage In / Garbage Out. We have to question ourselves regularly as to what we are feeding our minds. If we feed our minds trash, trash will be the resulting behavior. Fantasy looks for a way to become reality. The longer we allow our thoughts to linger on the idea of an affair, the more likely the affair will materialize. The key is to recognize and control those kinds of thoughts before they overtake us. 2 Corinthians 10:5b says that we are to "take captive every thought to make it obedient to Christ." What a powerful verse! Every thought that enters our mind needs to be captured for Christ! Philippians 4:8 tells us, "whatever is true, whatever is noble, whatever is right, whatever is pure, whatever is lovely, whatever is admirable - if anything is excellent or praiseworthy - think about such things." This verse gives us a new saying, Christ-like In / Christ-like Out.

God not only wants us to remain pure and holy and maintain faithfulness to our spouse, He also wants to use that obedience for His greater good for others. Part of our motivation for purifying our minds is our understanding of **The Purpose Of God**. God reveals part of that purpose to us in Romans 16:19. He says, "Everyone has heard about your obedience, so that I am full of joy over you; but I want you to be wise about what is good, and innocent about what is evil." When a believer has an affair it not only affects him and his family, but it puts a black mark on the name of Christ for everyone one else who knows about it. Paul says that God desires our obedience, in part, because of the positive affect it will have on those who are watching us. Part of being a Christian is setting an example for others to follow. God has purposed in His heart that we remain faithful to our spouse, and by so doing, we show the world that what we believe is more than just words.

God says that He wants us to be "wise about what is good, and innocent about what is evil." Doesn't that sound like just the opposite of what is true for most of society today, and for that matter, much of the church? Let's stop for a minute and compare the number of Scripture verses we have committed to memory with the number of songs containing inappropriate language or themes that we know all the words to. How many television shows or movies have we seen that portrayed adulterous relationships? Compare those with the amount of time we spend studying God's Word or praying. It would appear that many of us are innocent about what is good, and wise about what is evil. This worldly knowledge and thinking can break down our principles and standards, making us vulnerable to Satan's temptations. God praises innocence, but the world in which we live ridicules it. The key is found in who we are trying to please.

Protect Ourselves

Regularly I listen to people try to explain to me and to their spouse why they chose to commit adultery. Most of those explanations sound the same. They say things like, "It's not like I went looking for an affair, it just happened," or "I don't know how it happened, I just woke up one day and was in over my head." Many an affair begins harmlessly enough. A glance, a smile, a giggle, a touch, a thought. Just because we don't go looking for an affair doesn't justify it when it happens. But it does scare me. I listen to people who believe in the Lord, are active in their church, love their spouse and children, and never dreamed they would betray them - and yet they did. How do we make sure that sad story is not ours one day? I believe there are several steps we can take to protect ourselves.

I have shared this plan with hundreds of people in my office. The only ones who seem to agree with me whole-heartedly are the ones who have already suffered defeat. Most of the others nod their heads politely, but don't really believe that these principles apply to them. Several have even told me that they think I am paranoid, and that this plan is far and above what is necessary. I wish they would talk to those who have walked down that destructive path and are now living to regret it. Read through the next few steps prayerfully, asking God if he would have you implement them into your own marriage.

Step # 1 - Beware: Never put yourself in a position to be tripped up.

In twenty eight years of marriage I have never promised my wife that I will not have an affair. I have told her that I don't ever want to do anything that would hurt our relationship. I have assured her that I love her and am not looking to be with anyone else. She knows that I am doing everything possible to never put myself in any compromising positions. She also knows that I pray regularly that God will help me stay committed to my marriage vows, and I ask her to pray for me regularly as well. I believe that to make a promise that I will never do something that I know good and well I am capable of doing is foolish and dangerous. And I believe it is the very thing Satan would want me to do.

1 Corinthians 10:12 says, "So, if you think you are standing firm, be careful that you don't fall." Pride is the precursor to destruction. When it comes to the topic of affairs, I cannot be so foolish as to believe that it could never happen to me. I have known and heard about men who walked close to God, men who were holy and sincere in their faith, men who loved their wife and family with all their heart, who have betrayed their marital vows and lost it all. If it could happen to them, then why not me? To think that I am so much more holy, so much closer to God than they were, is nothing but foolish pride. The truth is that I am just stupid enough to walk down that same path, and God, Satan, and I all three know it.

Recognizing my weaknesses and sinful tendencies makes me stronger and helps me keep up my defenses. If I don't believe that I am capable of adultery, then I won't be spending any time on my knees asking for God's help to keep me from it. When Satan hears any of us saying, "I know that will never happen to me," he begins to lick his lips and rub his hands together and make some plans to see just how serious we are. I have no desire to invite that kind of trouble.

Step # 2 - Be Safe: Never put yourself in a position to be tempted.

Everyone I know who has committed adultery put themselves in the wrong place at the wrong time with the wrong person. The Bible never tells us to stand and fight temptation, it tells us to run - run fast and run far. Too many of us think we are strong enough to go toe-to-toe with the devil. Think about that, we are willing to stand face-to-face and fight a roaring lion, the prince of this world, the father of all the demons. That doesn't sound very smart. And the end result is that we are left defeated, embarrassed, and alone.

For years I worked in student ministry, and I used to tell those teenagers that after they had picked up their date, driven down a dark, lonely road, parked, climbed into the back seat, and were misbehaving, was not the best time to pray, "God, help me not mess up!" The best time to pray was before the date ever began. And the prayer needed to be, "God, help me not to drive my date down a dark, lonely road, park, climb into the back seat, and mis-behave." We can't put ourselves in a position to mess up and then hope we are strong enough not to! That is foolish.

Affairs begin innocently enough. First, we meet each other at work. Then we stop by each other's desk every now and then just to talk. Soon we realize that the other person laughs at all our jokes, really listens when we talk, seems to genuinely care for us, and looks forward to our time together. After a while we begin to see that we have so much in common, more than we do with our spouse. We find ourselves thinking about them all day long - the way they look, the way they smell, the way they act. One day we decide to have lunch together, just the two of us. We enjoy talking to each other so much that we exchange cell phone numbers so we can talk more as we each drive home from work. Our conversations turn from friendly chit-chat to gripe sessions about our troubled marriages to intimate conversations about what we would like to do together. Soon we devise a plan to fulfill those longings. And before we know it we are in the midst of a full fledged affair, jeopardizing everything we have ever cared about in the process.

When we play with fire we get burned. We need to be very careful with opposite sex friendships. We can never share intimate marital details or marriage problems with anyone of the opposite sex. When we allow ourselves to be put in compromising positions the chances of us blowing it are strong. Accountability is a necessity. We need to find someone we trust and ask them to keep us accountable. Ephesians 5:3 tells us that "among you there must not be even a hint of sexual immorality. "Not even a hint! Remember, there is no such thing as a little harmless flirting or innocent attention. We must do everything within our power to avoid situations that could prove to be harmful.

Step # 3 - Be Smart: Never put yourself in a position to be talked about.

This is the one where I lose most people. They try to hang with me to this point, but then they just look at me like I am being ridiculously paranoid. I don't believe that I am. The Bible has much to say about this topic. We are to live a life that is above reproach. Our character and lifestyle should reflect our faith in Christ. We are to never cause anyone to stumble because of our behavior. Others are to see our good deeds and glorify our Father in heaven. People tell me all the time, "I don't care what others think about me." Well I don't see why not, because it sure seems important to God! If our character and reputation are not important to us, what is?

I Thessalonians 5:22 says that we are to "avoid every appearance of evil" It is not enough that we avoid doing wrong, we need to avoid anything that even looks wrong. After all, we don't even have to do anything wrong to hurt our reputation, all it takes is for enough people to think and say that we have done wrong. For twenty eight years Pamela and I have made a pact with each other that we will never be alone with a member of the opposite sex. That means that I don't go to lunch alone with another woman, I don't ride in the car alone with another woman, I do not visit another woman alone at her house, I don't spend time on the phone with another woman, and I don't get into an e-mail relationship with another woman. Now, we do have the over 80 rule. If a woman in our church is over 80 years old, I can give her a ride or visit her in her home without even telling my wife. But, we have already discussed the fact that when I turn 70 that rule goes out the window!

People ask me, "So, does that mean that I can't have friends of the opposite sex?" For Pamela and I the answer is yes, that it exactly what that means. After all, what are we trying to protect, a friend-

ship or our marriage? I know all of this seems extreme - and it probably is. What's wrong with that? We have extreme sports and extreme make-overs, why can't we have extreme marriages? I know
it seems crude, but the fact is that if I am never alone with another
woman I guarantee I will not have sex with her! And that is the only
guarantee I have. Arch Hart made a comment several years ago
that I will never forget. He said, "Every man has his price." I know
that he is right. There is a woman, or type of woman, that would
make a man believe that she was worth sacrificing everything just
to have. Arch said that when you see her, run.

Partner Satisfaction

This last section covers a very touchy subject that needs to be
taken in context with the rest of this chapter and the book as a
whole. Adultery has no excuse, and no one who has committed
adultery can place the blame on their spouse. It was a choice they
made, a decision that they have to pay for. This section is not giving
adulterers an excuse for their behavior, but it is giving all of us who
have not experienced betrayal and are working hard at avoiding
that disaster, a plan to put in place that will help us achieve that
goal. 1 Corinthians 7:3-5 says:

> The husband should fulfill his marital duty to his wife, and like-
> wise the wife to her husband. The wife's body does not be-
> long to her alone but also to her husband. In the same way,
> the husband's body does not belong to him alone, but to his
> wife. Do not deprive each other except by mutual consent
> and for a time, so that you may devote yourselves to payer.

Then come together again so that Satan will not tempt you because of your lack of self-control.

The Scripture seems clear here that God's plan for marriage is that as husband and wife we make every effort to make sure that our spouse's sexual **Needs Are Met**. In a marriage relationship husband and wife are there to satisfy each other's needs, emotional and physical. This passage says that our bodies belong to each other, and that our spouse's body and theirs alone is where we are to turn to get those needs met. God's Word is filled with passages that tell us that we are to be satisfied with the spouse He has provided for us. God created a sexual desire within us and then provided us with a spouse to fulfill those desires. Clear communication is essential here. We need to communicate our needs to each other, and we need to hear and respond to the needs our spouse shares with us. Remember, we are to put each other's needs higher than our own, seeking always to please each other.

We want to please our spouse and fulfill their needs so that they are **Never Searching**. This passage says that depriving each other sexually can lead to temptation. We want to make sure that we are not doing anything that would cause our spouse to struggle more with temptation than they already do. We never want our spouse to go looking elsewhere for what he/she should be finding at home. This is all part of God's plan for marriage.

Having said all of this I need to stop and insert an very large BUT. We should meet each other's needs, and we don't want our spouse to look elsewhere, but no matter what, there are **No Excuses!** Many people have affairs even when the sex at home is very good. Adultery is about so much more than sex. It is about attention and affection and connection. But mostly it's about selfishness. No one can ever use the excuse that they went out and had an affair because they weren't getting enough sex at home. The fact is that if we never had sex again with our spouse for the rest of our marriage, we would still not have a valid excuse for adultery! Remember where we started this chapter - "You shall not commit adultery." Period. Yes we strive to meet each other's needs. Yes our bodies belong to each other. Yes we have an obligation to fulfill our spouse's sexual desires. But even when those things do not happen, we are still held responsible for our marital faithfulness. And God will accept nothing less.

But what if it's too late for your marriage? What if you or your spouse have already blown it, and now you are reeling from the affects? If that is true for you then you both need help. You need ongoing couple counseling and time to heal. There are some helpful books you could read and work through. *Torn Asunder*[1] is an excellent resource that also has an accompanying workbook. *Surviving Betrayal*[2] is a great tool that will allow you to work together through your pain. Also, *His Needs / Her Needs*[3] covers this topic in the first section of the book. Please get help, and don't give up. Our God is a big God. Remember, "I can do everything through Him who gives me strength." (Philippians 4:13)

Chapter 10

CHILDREN

This chapter is all about the affect children have on a marriage. It seems that just about the time we begin to figure this whole marriage deal out, God blesses us with an addition, and everything changes. Our perspective changes, our priorities change, our finances change, and our relationship with each other changes. It doesn't take long before we can't even remember what life was like BC (before children). The problem is that one day this crazy life will bring us back around to where we started, just the two of us. If we are not successful navigating our years with the kids, we might find that we have very little left when they are gone.

Managing Time

From the very beginning it is obvious that children are no respecters of time. They come home from the hospital sleeping when it is light and wide awake all night long. Have you ever noticed that small children only throw up in the middle of the night? I don't think I can ever recall a time when my kids were hugging the toilet in broad day light. They are not good at giving the grown ups quiet time. Whenever we sit down to talk to each other we can be

assured of an interruption. Time was hard enough to manage before we had little ones. How do we do it now?

How do we make sure that each of us is getting a little quality
Individual Time? We all need some time when we can just be alone.
As believers it is essential that we have some alone time to spend
with God. For those of us who have been Christians for a while we
know the value of developing a consistent time and place for our
devotional. It may be the first thing in the morning or the last thing
at night, but consistency is the key. This is all fine and dandy before
kids, but what happens then? There is no such thing as a "regular"
time schedule, at least when they are younger. This can really put a
dent into our quiet time.

I wish there was a patented answer, but there's not. All I can say
is that we need each other's help to guard a little time each day for
us to spend with God. We need to develop a plan, work that plan
as best we can, and improvise when all else fails. We have already
discussed the importance of our individual walks with God when it
comes to the overall health of our marriage. This is not an area we
can afford to let slide. We need to do whatever it takes to protect
this time for ourselves and for our spouse.

We also need individual time with our thoughts. Many young
moms feel like their brains are mush at the end of a busy day with
energetic toddlers. As husbands, we need to make it a priority to
take those kids off her hands for a few minutes each day, allowing
her to do whatever it takes to refresh herself. And what about our
interests and hobbies? Do we just forgo all of that until we are empty nesters? I think a little time for golfing or fishing or tennis or reading

can be a healthy ingredient for a young family. In moderation, individual recreation can breathe into us the energy we need to keep going strong.

A second critical area that needs protecting is our **Couple Time**. We have already discussed the importance of talking and dating and praying together. Understanding the importance of these activities and having enough time to do them are two different issues. Something as simple as communication can become extremely difficult with small children. One great time for Pamela and I to talk is when we are in the car together. We have always enjoyed long talks when we go on long trips. We realized early on that those private conversations are almost impossible with a couple of pairs of ears straining to hear every word from the back seat. Even regular night time communication is strained as the children's bedtimes continually get later with age. Soon it is all we can do to muster up enough strength to say good night before we fall asleep. It may not be in the car, and it may not be at night, but we have to carve out some regular time for couple communication, or our marriage will suffer the consequences.

What about time for dating? Dating is easier to do before we have kids, but it is so much more important after they come along. Not only do we need the time away, time just to talk and laugh and remember why we fell in love in the first place, but our children need this time as well. They need to see us loving each other. They need to see us going off together, making each other a priority. There is no better way to develop security in our kids than to spend quality time with each other. That includes our sex life. The most difficult time in a marriage to grow intimately is when we are raising small children. They are exhausting, they interrupt, they can't sleep, they are thirsty, they are messy, and they can be very quiet when they sneak around. This is a great time to take advantage of locks on the bedroom door! We have to have private couple time.

We also need quality **Children Time**. As our children grow it is vital that each parent set aside some time for each child each month. Those times make our children feel special and loved. They can be as simple as an early morning breakfast or a trip to the baseball card shop. They can also be things like a candlelight dinner with our daughter or a ball game with our son. (Of course, girls like ball games too - but I probably wouldn't try the candlelight dinner thing with my boy. We would probably end up catching something on fire.) The important thing is that they have our undivided attention for that whole period of time. They get to talk about whatever they want to talk about. I have learned more about my kids during those "date" times than probably any other. We can also use those times to talk about some of the topics we want to discuss. These are great teachable moments. Special times together meet their needs and mold their character. We need to take advantage of these times when our children are small, because they are harder to come by the older they get. Some of my favorite individual times still to this day are sitting on the edge of the bed right before they go to sleep. Some of the best conversations we have ever had were when we were sitting in the dark, winding down the day, listening to my kids share their heart. Not only will these times strengthen our relationship with our kids, but there is something about watching our spouse make our children a priority that strengthens the marriage as well.

A fourth area of time that needs to be managed is our **Family Time**. Making quality time together a priority is of the utmost importance. Family time is a time for talking and listening to each other. Times when the television is off and we are really focused on each other. Family times should be fun. We can play games together and laugh and sing and act crazy. We can go for walks and play sports and listen to music and do funny dances. The important part is that we are creating memories. Some family time can be spent learning. We can study the Bible together or read books out loud. We can go on field trips or family adventures. The most important aspect of family time is that we take time to show love to each other. We tell our children how much we love them, we show that love by our actions, as we just hug and kiss and wrestle and snuggle. I loved to watch my teenage son climb up in his mom's lap and just sit for a while. He was at least a foot taller than her already, but I hoped those days would never end. I have heard it said many times that it is not the quantity of time that matters, but the quality. I believe that is a lie that some dad made up to ease his conscience for being too busy. Good family time is both quality and quantity.

Measuring Tension

The result of trying to manage all four of these time areas is tension - pressure! Children are a wonderful gift from God, but they can also add stress to our already busy lives. It is easy to find ourselves exhausted and edgy at the end of a long day. Our bodies are worn out and our patience is thin. With that scenario it doesn't take much to push us to the breaking point. How do we handle our conflict that is brought on as a result of having children?

Sometimes we are **Arguing Because Of The Children**. When couples come in for counseling one of the top sources of conflict they list is the kids. There are several reasons for this. Children may be small, but they are smarter than they look. They learn at an early age how to play one parent against the other. We have to work hard to not allow that to happen. Standing together as one is the most important, and yet the most difficult aspect of parenting. If we don't master this essential parenting skill, they will eat us alive! A united front is sometimes difficult because we come into marriage with different philosophies of child-rearing. We come from different backgrounds and were raised differently. This is a big enough issue in a first marriage, but it is even more complicated in blended families. In those cases the parenting plan has already been put in place, and now someone new is being added to the mix, someone who has their own unique ways. It is very unfair, but sometimes we find ourselves arguing with each other over completely separate issues, but blaming the kids because it is easier than dealing with the real problems. The children are only the presenting problem, but digging any deeper to get to the true source of the trouble may be more painful than we are willing to endure.

It is easy to get into the habit of **Arguing In Front Of The Children**. Personally, I do not believe it is always wrong to disagree in front of our kids. They learn how to argue by watching us (scary thought, isn't it?). If we have a good marriage with healthy conflict resolution skills in place, our children can learn from our disagreements. What if our kids never see us argue? They may grow up to falsely believe that couples who love each other should never disagree. After all, they never saw their parents in conflict. If they enter marriage with this idea, they will quickly become disillusioned and frustrated, feeling like their own marriage is a failure. On the other hand, what if they watch us argue and fight all the time, but they never get the opportunity to see us work through it? If we argue in front of them, and yet make up behind closed doors, they may falsely assume that couples can fuss and fight and just go to bed and everything will automatically be better in the morning. If they never watch us work through conflict, they will struggle with handling it themselves. They may develop the mentality that we can hurt people and it will just go away with a little time. It is alright if they see us disagreeing, but they also need to see us apologizing and making up. Now hear me, I am saying it is fine if our kids watch us disagree periodically and struggle through our conflict. I am not saying that it is healthy for them to watch us scream and yell and name call and be nasty. That is destructive and never acceptable! Also, we never want to argue about the kids in front of the kids. Those discussions should always be private.

If we are not careful we will fall into a pattern of **Arguing With The Children**. It is unhealthy for our family and for our marriage when we fuss and fight with the kids. It is a source of constant pressure and frustration. We want to develop a good communication system where we can voice our complaints, while at the same time being respectable to each other. Our home should not be a war zone. We want to stand united as parents, but we do not want to gang up on our kids. We can also find ourselves turning on each other when one parent is correcting a child and the other one is defending him. As partners we need to talk with each other, calm each other down, help ease the tension, and defend each other to our children. Sometimes we need to gently pull our spouse aside and give him/her a chance to take a breather, and see things from a clearer perspective. The Scriptures tell us not to exasperate our kids. An environment of tension and conflict is exasperating. We need to make sure that we are not taking out our frustrations with each other on our kids, and make sure we are not taking out our frustrations with our kids on each other.

Maintaining Togetherness

The only way to survive and thrive throughout the child-rearing years is to go through it all together. We have to remind ourselves regularly that we were a couple before the kids came along and we will be a couple again after they are gone. Our job is to stand hand-in-hand and grow up our children into God-loving, well adjusted, healthy adults. In the process we have to fight to make sure that we don't take our focus off each other. When our children were little Wayne Watson came out with his tear-jerking song, *Water Color Ponies*. The chorus of that song says, "Baby what will we do when it comes back to me and you?" That's a good question. And if we are not making that a priority right now, it will be a difficult transition then.

We need to concentrate on **Working Together**. Again, we cannot allow our children to pit us against each other. We are raising our family as a team, not two separate individuals. We may not always agree with our spouse's parenting style, and we have the right to sit down and discuss these issues with each other, but we must show mutual respect for the parenting role. If we get the idea that "I am the better parent," our relationship will suffer, and the kids will jump on board and use it against us. One rule of thumb is to never correct or put each other down in front of the kids. When we do so we ruin the other spouse's credibility. They deserve more respect than that. Another temptation we must fight is the urge to triangle our kids, using them to back us up in a disagreement. If Pamela and I are disagreeing about something that happened a few days before, it is not fair for either of us to pull Jeremiah or Abigail into the discussion, hoping they will defend our point of view.

We will not always agree with every parental decision our spouse makes, but we can never question those decisions in front of the kids. They have to see a united front. Even if we are in total disagreement, we need to keep our opinions to ourselves until we can get alone. Then we can share our point of view and have a healthy discussion. If our spouse is determined to defend their position then we must stand behind them. If they change their stance, we must let them go back to the children with the change of plans. If we go behind closed doors, discuss the situation, and can come out on the same page, our marriage and our kids will be better off for it.

Our children also need to see us **Loving Together**. I have heard it said so many times, and I couldn't agree more, the best thing we can do for our kids is to love each other. We are in love, and our children need to see it. They need to see us showing affection, and spending time together, and modeling our loving relationship. They need to hear us verbally express that love regularly. We are best friends, lovers, and soul mates. If we believe that those are good things, things that we desire for our children one day, we need to let them in on it and show them how to love. Our children will model what they see more than what they are taught. John Maxwell tells a story that illustrates this point:

> We've stressed with both kids how important it will be for them to love their spouse when they get married. But we know that just telling them isn't enough; they also have to see it. Margaret and I have always been affectionate with one another, and we've never hidden that from the children. One day when Joel Porter was about six years old, Margaret and I were in the kitchen, kissing. He came bursting in, and when he saw us he said, "Are you guys falling in love all over again?' Even at that age he understood how we felt about each other.[1]

Probably the most important aspect of togetherness we need to fight for is the promise of **Staying Together**. Matthew 19:6 says, "they are no longer two, but one.

Therefore, what God has joined together, let man not separate." This whole togetherness deal is designed to last an entire lifetime. One of the best gifts we can ever give to our children is the security that comes from knowing that we are not going to allow anything to break up our marriage. A large portion of their friends are from broken homes, and the fear of parental divorce can be debilitating. Ross Campbell says, "the most important relationship in the home is the marriage bond, which takes primacy over the parent-child relationship. The security of a teenager and the quality of the parent-child bonding are largely dependent on the quality of the marital bonding."[2] Not only do we owe our children a secure home, we also owe them a stable home. Many kids grow up in an environment of instability and confusion. One day there is happiness and the next there is turmoil. Together we must work to make a home marked by peace and serenity. Our children will never feel secure in our promise of a life-time commitment if we don't believe it ourselves. The more in love we are, the more committed we are to each other, and the more we allow that love and commitment to permeate our home, the healthier our kids will be.

CONCLUSION

Marriage is hard work. I don't think that can be denied. The real question for all of us is, "How hard are we willing to work to make our marriages successful?" Reading a relationship book can make the task seem daunting. Each chapter reminds us of another area that needs our constant attention. Like the art of plate spinning, every time we get one area going well another one begins to fall apart. The whole process can be exhausting. If we are not careful the thought of giving up can raise its ugly head. We have already looked at the statistics and they are not pretty. So what is the answer?

We have to have hope; hope that a marriage can last a lifetime. We have to have faith; faith in God, in ourselves, and in each other. We have to always put our spouse's needs ahead of our own and strive for what is best for them. We must resist the slippery slide into negativism, criticism, judgmentalism, and all the other hurtful isms! We cannot give up when the going gets tough. We must give 100% 100% of the time.

But it has got to be more than just trying to prevent our relationships from crashing and burning. We cannot just work hard at preventing the negative, but we must find a way to accentuate the positive. Marriage is a beautiful gift from God! He has given us a helpmate, a best friend, a lover, and a partner for life. This relationship is meant to be celebrated and cherished and nourished every day. When we do so it will grow.

The truth is that the heath of our marital relationship is really up to us. We can blame each other, society, our parents, or even God when we are hurting and lonely and discouraged. We can make excuses for all of the hurt feelings, painful experiences, missed opportunities and broken hearts, or we can take ownership of them. If it is true that the only person we can really change is ourselves, then that is probably a good place to start.

I hope that *Marriage in Motion* will help you along your marital journey. I pray that God will use some of the Biblical principles, practical applications, or personal stories to encourage and strengthen you. The process is difficult but the destination is worth it.

ENDNOTES

Chapter One

1. Les and Leslie Parrott, Saving Your Marriage Before It Starts (Grand Rapids, MI: Zondervan Publishing House, 1995), 135.

2. David and Jan Stoop, When Couples Pray Together (Ann Arbor, MI: Vine Books, 2000), 25.

3. Ibid., 25

4. Parrott, Saving Your Marriage, 135.

5. John Gottman, Why Marriages Succeed or Fail (New York, NY: Fireside Books: Simon & Schuster, 1994), 16.

6. O. Palmer Robertson, The Christ of the Covenants (New Jersey: Presbyterian & Reformed Publishing Co., 1980), 7.

7. Jim Smoke, Growing Through Divorce (Eugene: Harvest House Publishers, 1995), 53.

Chapter Two

1. Mary Stewart Van Leeuwen, Gender and Grace (Downers Grove, Illinois: InterVarsity Press, 1990), 77.

2. Willard J. Harley, Jr., His Needs / Her Needs (Grand Rapids: Fleming H. Revell, 2001)

3. Mels Carbonell, Uniquely You (Blue Ridge, Georgia).

4. Larry Crabb, Men and Women (Grand Rapids: Zondervan Publishing House, 1991),153.

Chapter Three

1. Martin E.P. Seligman, Learned Optimism (New York: Simon & Schuster, 1998), 20.

2. John Gottman, Why Marriages Succeed Or Fail (New York: Simon & Schuster, 1994), 73.

3. Gary Chapman, The Five Love Languages (Chicago: Northfield Publishing, 1995)

4. John Ortberg, The Life You've Always Wanted (Grand Rapids: Zondervan Publishing House, 1997), 64.

5. Henri Nouwen, The Return of the Prodigal Son (New York: Doubleday Publishing, 1994), 42.

6. Neil Clark Warren, Make Anger Your Ally (Colorado Springs: Focus On The Family Publishing, 1990), 18-19.

Chapter Four

1. Gary Chapman, The Five Love Languages Video Pack (Nashville: Life-Way Press, 1995).

Chapter Five

1.   http://www.divorcestatistics.info/divorce-statistics-and-divorce-rate-in-the-usa.html.

2. Les and Leslie Parrott, Saving Your Marriage Before It Starts (Grand Rapids: Zondervan Publishing House, 1995), 113.

Chapter Six

1. Cameron Lee, PK: Helping Pastor's Kids Through Their Identity Crisis (Grand Rapids: Zondervan Publishing House, 1992), 145-146.

2. Lewis B. Smedes, The Art Of Forgiving (Nashville: Moorings, 1996), xiii.

3. Les Carter & Frank Minirth, The Choosing To Forgive Workbook (Nashville: Thomas Nelson Publishers, 1997),17.

4. Ibid., 8

5. Neil Clark Warren, Make Anger Your Ally (Colorado Springs: Focus On The Family Publishing, 1990), 6-7.

Chapter Seven

1. R.J. Sternberg, A Triangular Theory of Love, Psychological Review. 1986. 93, 119-135.

2. David and Jan Stoop, When Couples Pray Together (Ann Arbor: Vine Books, 2000), 25.

3. Ibid., 25.

4. Les and Leslie Parrott, Saving Your Marriage Before It Starts (Grand Rapids: Zondervan Publishing House, 1995), 145.

5. Jack and Judith Balswick, The Family: A Christian Perspective on the Contemporary Home (Grand Rapids: Baker Books, 1989), 31.

Chapter Eight

1. Jack and Judith Balswick, The Family: A Christian Perspective on the Contemporary Home (Grand Rapids: Baker Books, 1989).

Chapter Nine

1. Dave Carder, Torn Asunder (Chicago: Moody Press, 1992).

2. Donald R. Harvey, Surviving Betrayal (Grand Rapids: Baker Books, 1995).

3. Willard J. Harley, Jr., His Needs / Her Needs (Grand Rapids: Fleming H. Revell, 2001)

Chapter Ten

1. John C. Maxwell, Breakthrough Parenting (Colorado Springs: Focus On The Family Publishing, 1996), 85.

2. Ross Campbell, How To Really Love Your Teenager (Colorado Springs: Chariot Victor Publishing, 1981), 19.

ABOUT THE AUTHOR

Dr. John P. Hobbs is the Pastor of Care and Counseling at Crossroads Church in Newnan, Georgia. His responsibilities include overseeing marriage counseling, training lay counselors, and developing support groups. He holds degrees from Columbia Bible College, New Orleans Baptist Theological Seminary, and Fuller Theological Seminary. John and his wife have two children.

CPSIA information can be obtained at www.ICGtesting.com
Printed in the USA
BVOW04s2240021013

332787BV00001B/72/P